ISBN: 978-1-4497-5014-5 (hc)
ISBN: 978-1-4497-5015-2 (sc)
ISBN: 978-1-4497-5016-9 (e)

Library of Congress Control Number: 2012907899

WestBow Press books may be ordered through booksellers or by contacting:

WestBow Press
A Division of Thomas Nelson
1663 Liberty Drive
Bloomington, IN 47403
www.westbowpress.com
1-(866) 928-1240

Printed in the United States of America

WestBow Press rev. date: 05/17/2012

FROM DOPE
TO HOPE

Kevin Hodge

WestBow
PRESS
A DIVISION OF THOMAS NELSON

To the awesome God I serve who has inspired me to write this book. I am truly grateful to Him.

To my wife, Tonia, for her love and continued support; my grandmother, Ruby Brown, for her unconditional love; to all of my children, whom I pray will continue to look to God for all of their needs, and to my editor, Minister Danita Hammock, for her help and encouragement throughout the writing of this book.

To the many people who aided me along my journey: I thank you all and pray for your continued strength in the Lord.

CONTENTS

FOREWORD

Kevin Hodge is an unusually gifted young man with extraordinary talents. He came up on the rough side of the mountain but because of his faith in God and his unusual determination to succeed, he never stayed down but always got back up again. He kept on "trucking" in Christ.

He is called of God as a street Evangelist, as one of the best. He knows how to speak to the heart of the wayward that makes them listen and surrender their lives to Christ.

I have known Kevin since he was a seventeen years old young man up until this present time. He is an excellent example of how to suffer outrageous fate and still keep standing. He has suffered horrendous blows but yet keeps on stepping in the footsteps of Jesus Christ.

Read his story, be strengthened, be encouraged and be blessed.

Gratefully yours,
Reverend John L. Scott, His Pastor

PREFACE

I never had any idea that all of the pain and suffering I've gone through could possibly be used to help someone else. If you would have told me that I would write a life-story book with the sole purpose of encouraging someone else, I would have called you crazy.

Although the trauma in my life was often excruciatingly painful and life threatening, God saw me through it all. He has allowed me to survive and strive in spite of it all.

There are many very good motivational and inspirational books on the market today. But I have not yet read one that exposes suffering, abuse, and addiction as I attempt to do here. It is only by God's amazing grace that I am sharing my in-depth experience, as, on my own, I would not be willing to share my bad habits, struggles, and ungodly behavior. However, God has touched my heart in such a way that I have revealed and shared all my truths with you. There is nothing hidden that will not be exposed.

My earnest hope and prayer is that someone will be drawn closer to the almighty love of God through my story. I also pray that someone in need of help will find the same power that transformed my life from dope to hope.

This is my story.

chapter 1

THE EARLY YEARS

Looking back on my years growing up in Harlem, one of the first things I remember is running down the stairs wearing my brother's big shoes. I'll never forget my panic as the police rushed upstairs to my apartment. I would later learn that my mother suffered a nervous breakdown and would be institutionalized for the next three years. I remember having to leave a lot of my favorite toys and clothes as we were moved to my Grandmother's house to live for the next few years. Grandmother did not live too far away, but the event was shocking and traumatic for me.

Kenny and Kim, my brother and sister, seemed to adapt well to the drastic change, but I was in a great deal of pain for a six-year-old. Mom had been taken from me. This meant that I had to be transferred to another school. Now I would have to meet new students and be tested to find out how smart I was or wasn't. I was very afraid of my Grandfather. He was a big man who spoke loudly and with much authority. Grandmother wasn't so bad, but she, like Grandfather, knew how to handle that brown leather belt. I really missed Mom and often wondered where she was and if I would ever see her again. I also asked myself, "Where is Dad?"

I never knew my dad, but as I grew older, I began to question his whereabouts. Watching most of the other kids go out with their parents while we went out with our Grandparents felt kind of strange to me. Dad was very much alive, but he just wasn't in the picture.

Kenny, the oldest, looked out closely for Kim and me. I recall walking through Saint Nicholas Park to visit Dad. I had many questions, but I was afraid to ask them. The first question was why he didn't take us instead of letting Grandmother and Grandfather take care of us. Yeah, he gave us a few dollars here and there, but what I really needed was fatherly nurturing. I needed a male figure to teach and instruct me in the ways of life. Grandfather played with us but that was different. He was very strict, strong, and tough, but he wasn't Dad.

Second Grade for Life

I loved school because it was my way out. It was my opportunity to get away from Kenny and Kim as well as my grandparents and was a relief. I was in a new school with a new teacher and new students. When I look back on those years, I now believe that I was a real problem child. My grandparents bought me glasses because of my bad eyesight. Every time they bought me a pair, I broke them. Obviously I had a problem. I just didn't want to wear them, so I kept breaking them. It didn't take them long to realize what I was doing, and soon I was the only second grader with taped eyeglasses.

I was enjoying the second grade like everyone else until something happened that changed my life forever. There was another student in my class who lived one block away from me. Although she was a girl, she had boyish ways about her. I guess that's how we connected. We were always told to go straight home after school. We then would have a snack and proceed with our homework assignments. This one particular day, my friend asked me to walk her home. She assured me that I would not be long and would get home before being classified as late. I walked her home, and she invited me to come up. She had an older brother who upon our arrival sent her to the store or somewhere. He then offered me a sandwich. Peanut butter and jelly was very popular back then. The next thing I remember is that he was sodomizing me. I cried, screamed, and begged him to stop, but he would not.

I was seven years old and did not have a clue as to what was happening to me. I was traumatized. I never told anyone, because I was too afraid that I would be blamed for going home with my friend that day.

I wrote this poem years later, but no words can describe the pain I felt at the time.

"Nobody Knows the Hurt"

Nobody knows the hurt that one could feel inside
Nobody knows the pain, for there's so many ways to hide
Nobody knows the pain and feeling of being rejected
Despite being well known, famous, or respected
It's a hurt that causes the strongest to become feeble and weak
It can snatch an individual off of his highest peak
So try to be more sensitive, observant, and alert
'Cause underneath the biggest smile or grin
Nobody knows the hurt.

My Grandparents made sure that Kenny, Kim, and I were dressed well. Church was a must for all who lived in 466 West

150th Street, Apartment 4F. All except for Grandfather. No one could make Grandfather do anything he didn't want to do. But every Sunday, the rest of us attended church and Sunday school. Kenny taught me how to play hooky from Sunday School. We would go to the Battle Grounds Park up the block but were back in church before Grandmother arrived for choir rehearsal. I would later learn of the powerful impact that church had on my life. I truly believe that I learned to read at church.

Grandfather proved his manhood to me years later when Kenny, Kim, and I went back to stay with Mom. She had just come home from the mental institution and lived in a one-room apartment. When I say one room, I mean one room. Mom had a boyfriend, which meant that she slept with him in the full-sized bed while Kenny, Kim, and I slept in the small fold-up bed. This was a very rough time in my life. Mom was in a deep depression and turned to alcohol to soothe her pain.

Just about every day, Mom's boyfriend got her good and drunk and then beat the hell out of her. The police constantly came to the house and escorted him out, but he only came back and resumed his actions. He will never know how much pain he caused our family. I thought often about trying to locate him, but God's grace would not allow me to do so. I still would like just to talk to him. My Grandparents always came to the rescue. Grandfather wanted desperately to kick his behind and really hurt him. I don't know how Grandfather managed not to hurt him. It must have been God at work restraining him.

I was about ten years old at the time, and these events had a disastrous impact on my academics. I didn't do well in school, so I was held over in the fifth grade. I had just transferred to another school and was afraid of the change. Sometimes I didn't go to sleep until one or two o'clock in the morning. I didn't even try to do well in school. I was a very sad young man.

I now realize the cause of some of my reckless living. Those years in the one-bedroom apartment were probably the worst years of my life. I wore clothes that brought a lot of attention to me, and classmates would often talk about my clothes and my eye. It wasn't my fault that I was born cross-eyed.

I had the best fifth-grade teacher that a student could possibly want. She was like a mother to me. She showed genuine concern for each student. In her class, I learned the multiplication table. She offered me and another student five dollars to stand in front of the class and recite our tables. After one month, I had to stand in front of the class to answer any multiplication problem, and I answered every question successfully. My friend Anthony Jones and I each earned five bucks. That was a bright light in the midst of darkness.

My fifth-grade teacher requested all students to visit the Hayden Planetarium at the Museum of Natural History on several Saturdays. One Saturday, I decided to visit with my sister and a fellow classmate, Matt. We were having a good time when my sister decided to ask two white boys for money. She did it, so I thought that I could too. She asked for a dollar and got it, so I asked for a quarter. I don't know if Matt asked for anything, but I know we were all arrested and charged with robbery. I was only ten years old when I committed my first crime. What a young age to start! We were all given probation and a hellacious butt whipping.

Mom's depression continued and so did her abuse. About this time, I recall memories of my Aunt Betty. Betty was Mom's drinking partner, but she was never around when Mom got slapped and knocked around. I was scarred because of my childhood.

At this point, I met two fine girls who were nice to me. First, I started going out with Donna. She was light-skinned and very gentle and kind to me. Then, in my fifth-grade class, I met Jackie. Jackie was brown-skinned and a nice, slender chick. She was very stern and demanding. I think that I was even afraid of her to some degree. Jackie found out about Donna, but Donna already knew about Jackie and was okay with it. Those girls really helped me a lot. My second year in the fifth grade wasn't too bad.

I was later placed in a low-academic-performing sixth-grade class for the rest of the school year. I was then told I would need to repeat the sixth grade. They said they would allow me to walk in graduation but that I would have to return to the sixth grade. I chose not to walk.

When I was eleven, we moved to a larger apartment in Grant Projects. We now had our own room and high-rise beds. The Grant Projects experience was much better, although Mom's drinking continued to increase. Eventually, Mom was admitted into Roosevelt Hospital, where she was to undergo open-heart surgery. I remember this so well because I went with her to the hospital, but I didn't realize that I would be coming home alone. I cried on my way back to the train station. I didn't know that open-heart surgery was such a serious operation.

Mom was in the hospital for her birthday. Her boyfriend came by while the family was visiting and gave her a card with a crisp fifty-dollar bill inside. We were so excited for her. I later found out that he came back for the money after we left. He was only putting on a front for the family.

Soon I was selling newspapers and packing groceries to make a few extra dollars because we rarely got allowance, and I became very independent. I really enjoyed working and earning my own money. There were several old ladies who always gave me a pretty decent tip. Most of my customers were opening their doors before I even shouted, "Paper!" They knew exactly what time I was coming. Packing groceries was very good training for me. I learned how to be humble and courteous. After all, I wanted a nice tip for my work and service. Working as a young man will always be something that I am grateful for. I have learned the essence of providing good service to others. It definitely pays off.

One thing I don't recall is being close to Kenny or Kim. I often seemed to be in my own world. I remember a fight I had with Kim, who was rough and didn't take any mess from me. One Christmas, I was so fortunate to get an Electro-Shot Shooting Gallery game—truly the best game I ever had. Kim wanted to take over the game, so she offered me some of her toys, but I would not budge. She became furious and tried to take over my game, but I wasn't having it. We then had a vicious fight, and I punched her with all my might. She in turn bit me on my arm with all of hers. Mom broke up the fight, but it was too late. Kim had left me with a scar that I still carry to this day. We now laugh about the incident.

Kenny was a tremendous strength for me in my early years. He sold newspapers and worked part-time at the local supermarket and shared his wealth with Kim and me. He brought candy home from the supermarket that he shared with us. Kenny carried a heavy load of responsibility as the oldest child. He too witnessed the abuse of our mother by a man twice his size and three times his age. Kenny made sure that Kim and I were always okay. He picked us up from school and took us to the after school program. He never let anyone mess with his little brother and sister. Kenny also made sure that I was dressed appropriately. When I look back on those rough times, I thank God for keeping us together. I recognize that so many families experience tougher circumstances than my family did.

One advantage for me when we moved to Grant Projects was that I quickly made friends with several of my neighbors. We played barrel ball and marshmallow freeze tag. We threw snowballs at buses and at people. I was a very wild young man, and my friends admired my courage. One of my closest friends, Chuck, and I would ride our bikes all over Manhattan and had a lot of fun together. Chuck and the other boys always talked about my mother's drinking problem. She really embarrassed Kim and me. Kenny was never around to be humiliated by Ma's behavior, although he knew that she had a serious problem.

But I had several problems at my new school with the other students. Some of the other boys thought it was a good opportunity to test me to see if I had any fighting skills. I had several fights but soon established myself and had no more problems.

I don't recall doing a great deal of work in class or at home. I was busy playing games and trying to make friends. The Ralph Burch School that I attended went up to grade six, so I spent many nights thinking long and hard about what would happen when I attended junior high school.

I missed my friends from 133rd Street as well as my dog, Tippy, whom I walked quite often when I was being punished for misbehaving. Tippy was my way out of the house; I would remind my mother that Tippy needed to be walked. When we moved, though, Tippy could not come along, because dogs were not allowed in the projects, so she had to be taken to the ASPCA to be put to rest. I was so hurt, but there was nothing I could do. I cried for my pet dog and was comforted by my grandfather, who had taken Tippy to the ASPCA.

Life for me began to take on a new meaning in the summer of 1973. One great thing that occurred as a result of our moving was that I got my first real job. I was walking down 125th Street and decided to buy an Icee at the Steak and Take Restaurant. As I waited for the man to scoop my cherry icy into the little cup, the owner approached me and asked me if I wanted a job. "Yes!" I said before I even knew how much I would be paid or what the hours would be. I don't recall for sure, but I think that my wages were fifteen cents an hour plus a free lunch. I was very excited and proud of myself.

The owner of the Steak and Take was Muslim and tried to convert me to Islam. He often talked about the white man as being the devil. I listened and learned a lot but never attended a service at the mosque. I wanted to go but it just never happened. I thank God now because I realize he had a better plan in store for me.

I really enjoyed working at the Steak and Take. I soon was promoted to cleaning and cooking the fish 'n' chip dinners. Some of the customers wondered who the new kid was and thought I had a lot of nerve coming into their neighborhood and taking their job.

The job was a great learning experience for me. The owner continued inviting me to the mosque and began harassing me so much about becoming a Muslim that I decided it was time to move on. Soon after I left, the business shut down and never reopened. The newspaper route was still holding up pretty well, and I also worked in the supermarket on Saturdays.

Kim also worked in the supermarket packing bags and made more money than I did. She understood the importance of a good education at a very early age and was the top learner in our home. Kim had a child at a very young age but still pursued and obtained her dreams. It's amazing that she endured the same pain and suffering that I did and yet turned out so different and became so educated

Ma started playing numbers on a daily basis. I remembered that check days were the third and the eighteenth of every month. Ma loved welfare. She was eligible and truly in need of their services. I remember her taking me with her to the face-to-face meetings.

Ma and I were very close yet very distant. I think that she sensed that I was in a lot of pain, but she just didn't know how to talk to me. She had her own issues and struggles in life. Life was a serious struggle for us as we just tried to keep our heads above water. We never talked about her time in the state mental hospital or how we fared with our grandparents. I don't think that my grandparents cared for Ma; they just tolerated her. Ma knew that they definitely didn't care for her lifestyle.

chapter 2
TOO HIGH FOR JUNIOR HIGH

I met a young lady at school named Tracy, who lived on the other side of Grant Projects. She was the serious joint. We often went to the movies and had a good time. When it was time for me to go upstairs at night, the first thing I would do is call Tracy. We would talk until Ma said that it was time for bed. I really, really liked her. I learned how to French kiss that summer; Tracy taught me well. She was also developing nicely, so I had something to hold on to. Tracy lived on the other side of Grant Projects, and I really didn't care for those cats on the other side. I almost had a few fights but some of my sixth grade classmates lived on that side so I was okay.

That summer went by fast, and soon it was time for school again. Back in those days, our topic of discussion was, "What are you getting for the first day of school?" That year Ma did a little better, and I got a leather coat. I was ready.

After two years in fifth grade and a portion of the sixth grade spent in two different schools, I graduated to junior high school. I wanted to get into a school outside of that district.

Sixth-grade graduation was one to be remembered. My favorite aunt, Tee, came from as far as Augusta, Georgia. I don't recall where we ate, but I do remember receiving a nice amount of money. I was a happy camper. That summer, I thought a great deal more about junior high school.

My teacher's name was Ms. Ryan. We sure gave her a hard way to go. I guess I thought that junior high school was a big game. I didn't focus on work at all. All that I remember is laughing and joking and being chased by someone. I don't remember one test that I took or homework assignment I completed. Seventh grade was not as hard, because I wasn't academically present. I was physically present, but that was as far as it went.

There were many fights between the blacks and Hispanics. I was never involved, but I always knew what was about to go down.

I had several friends at Stitt Junior High School uptown in Washington Heights, and we used to snap, or make fun of other people. It was only because of my past experience that I learned to snap on others. When I was in elementary school, everyone always talked about my attire. I had a fake leather coat, and boy, did they talk about that coat. I was also born cross-eyed, which others made fun of. I learned to take the insults, which helped harden my exterior. For those reasons, I learned to play the dozens. The dozens was a game where one would talk about another person's mother and the two playing would go back and forth making ill comments about each other's mother.well and fast. I became one of the best snappers in the whole school.

There was only one other person who could snap like me. His name was Ness. He took his name from the TV show *The Untouchables*. Ness was good, but I was better. We became friends by having snapping contests. We talked about each other's family as if they were dogs. Both our mothers were alcoholics, and we talked about our mothers like it was going out of style. We started hanging out and riding buses and being mischievous.

The school found out that my true address was different from what was on my record. I continued to state that I lived on 150th Street with my grandmother, but my assistant principal lived right across the street from me in Grant Projects. I was told that I had to either go to my zoned school or attend an alternative school. I chose the alternative school. The very first person I saw at the alternative school was Ness. I was thirteen years old.

The alternative school was a huge change in my life. I was in a setting with the worst of the worst students. I tried to do my best, but I became very uncooperative and unruly. Then I started drinking my mother's alcohol. It started out as a joke, but little did I know that I had started a habit that would be so hard to break. Ma loved her Smirnoff and grapefruit juice, and I started sipping a glass every now and then. I really felt good at the beginning but that soon changed. I continued in school but started cutting class and coming back late from lunch.

Kenny smoked pot almost daily and supplied my need. Just about everyone in school was smoking pot as well. We chipped in our money and purchased a three-dollar bag. All I had was fifteen cents, but they sure took it and used it for weed.

I was too high for junior high school. I started hanging on 123rd Street, where all kinds of drugs were being sold. I even started working for one of the basements and had all the smoke I wanted. I also got closer and closer to Ness, who was an experienced thief. He taught me well, and we stole bikes and skateboards. We stayed up late and hung with the big boys. I learned a lot of bad habits that took me a long time to break. We thought that we were so smart, but the reality is that we only cheated ourselves out of a much-needed education.

Ness went to Spofford Juvenile Correctional Facility for robbing someone, so I didn't see him for quite a while. But when he got out, we continued our way of life. We stole more bikes and smoked more pot all the way up until the eighth grade.

I don't recall how I was so inspired by Harold Melvin and the Blue Notes to write a poem as a result of their number-one hit "Wake up Everybody."

"Wake Up, Everybody"

Wake up everybody; it's a brand new day
Are you going to listen or try to walk away?
Wake up everybody, it's a different time
Walk always forward and do not look behind
Wake up everybody, do not be a fool
Get your education and try and school.

This was the first of many of my writings, but I should have taken heed to my own message. Eighth grade was coming to an end, and I needed to focus on high school. I chose the High School of Performing Arts because I had a knack for drama and because I met a drama teacher in seventh grade who really stirred me up. I didn't show it, though, because I wanted to be a tough guy. It was suggested to me that I recite a specific poem for my audition. I knew that I should have stuck with my own desire to recite "Ballad of the Landlord" by Langston Hughes. I failed the audition, and I was very upset with myself because once again I had been influenced by someone else.

I continued to steal Ma's liquor and thought that I really knew everything. At this time, my dad resurfaced. He was living on 155th and Nicholas Avenue, very close to my school, so I occasionally stopped by to pay him a visit. He worked in the Hunts Point Terminal Market and always brought home fruit. I guess that he knew I was getting older, because he offered me a joint or two. I continued to do poorly in school.

I had a very close friend, Eda, whom I had met in seventh grade. Eda was a cool guy, but he wasn't rowdy like me. Eda was quiet and smart. He did his homework and stayed out of trouble. I don't know how we became so close, but I think that he was one of the most positive people in my life.

When I heard that Eda was moving down South in the middle of the school year, I sneaked into the school to say good-bye to him but could not find him. After he moved away, I never saw him again. I cried and wrote a poem, "I Love My Friend." At the time, I didn't realize how much his absence affected me, and I never discussed it with anyone. I guess that it was just another loss that I carried, unknown even to myself. I believe that there are many people who, like me, carry scars from years past that have never experienced the freedom of healing.

The alternative school that I was placed in was called ACE and was located in what looked like an apartment building. One of the most influential instructors there was a guy I chose to call Cee. He was my homeroom teacher who spent the longest period of time with me and the other students. He was genuine; I guess that is why I liked him so much. He was down-to-earth and thought very highly of me. Some of the other students called me Teacher's Pet, I think because I began trying to get my work done. I really wanted to graduate that year. I guess for a short period of time I began to see the importance of learning.

It didn't last too long. Everyone talked about getting high on pot. I'll never forget one day in particular when just about every student came back from lunch stoned on pot. We all chipped in to buy a three-dollar bag of smoke. I remember so well because all I had was twenty-five cents, but the other students in the class took it, and we got a trey bag. The counselors knew we were stoned because we couldn't stop laughing.

There was one student named Mike (I called him Gay Mike because he acted very feminine). Mike always had money and was very upset because he was excluded that day. Mike had never smoked herb but wanted to desperately. Guess who took Mike to buy his first loose joint? You're right. Me. I didn't realize or even consider that Mike would not be able to conceal his state of mind. He laughed and talked so much that all the teachers knew he was on something. The teachers just didn't know how he was able to get the drugs. I was afraid that Mike would give away that I was the person responsible for supplying him with pot and that I hung out with him. One thing was for sure, everyone wanted to feel the way Mike was feeling.

We all believed that the counselors were smoking pot too, but we couldn't prove it. The end of the school year moved closer and closer, and I still didn't know which high school to choose. I have since learned to stick to what works for me. Someone once told me that you should never let someone else build your world, because they will always build it too small. I should have never let anyone change my decision, but I did, and it caused me a great deal of pain. Once again, I was rejected. I attempted to act like everything was okay, but deep down inside, I was wounded.

I began to think more about high school and how it would be for me. I had heard a great deal about it and really looked forward to a new environment and experience. We hardly went on any trips at ACE, and the setting was extremely different from regular school.

I recall one trip in particular. We went to a museum where there was a Black History exhibition. I recall this trip so vividly because the exhibit focused on a gentleman by the name of Paul Robinson. We learned about his many talents and athletic abilities. The trip was a really fun experience, and I think that many of the students really enjoyed it.

When we were about a block away from school, Dexter, another student, decided he wanted to fight me. I still don't know what it was that I did, but he wouldn't take no for an answer. When we were dismissed from school, Dexter waited right out front for me. The crowd immediately started instigating the fight, and I just couldn't get out of this one. I don't know why he wanted to fight, but Dexter ended up with a black and bleeding eye. After winning the fight, nobody messed with me for the remainder of the school year. That year proved to be an extremely trying year.

As we moved closer and closer to the end of the school year, more fights occurred, and several students were put out of the alternative school. One student named C-Boy was arrested and never returned.

My First Summer Job

As school came to an end, I began to focus on obtaining my first summer job. I was so excited. I looked forward to earning my own money and, most of all, buying my own school clothes. I went through the process of filling out all the paperwork. I even got to choose my own site. Many people were turned away, but I was very fortunate. My first check was only fifty dollars after three weeks of work, but I was promised another check at the end of the summer.

I worked in a tiny office on Broadway, where I met my good friend Jeff to the Left, whom I will speak about later. We were asked to protest about issues that I had no clue about. Jeff and I started shooting dice against each other—one of the talents I learned from my dad. I beat Jeff, and he owed me five dollars. I never thought that he would pay me, but he did. We became best friends over the summer as our jobs began to wind down.

I didn't think that I would see Jeff again. He was attending JFK High School, and I was going to Martin Luther King High School. I had given most of my money to Kenny to hold for me for new school clothes in September. I just knew I would be one of the flyest brothers in the school. But Kenny spent my money as quickly as I gave it to him. September came, and I had to wear his clothes. I was so upset, but there was nothing I could do, because Kenny was older and much bigger than me. I complained to Ma, but there was nothing she could do either. Kenny just got over on me like a fat rat, in other words he took advantage of me. I was so disappointed that I cried.

One thing that Kenny did do for me was supply my pot habit. Back in the day, we called it cheebah. A nice bag of cheebah was five dollars, or you could buy loose joints too. The joints were very skinny, but they did the job. My whole crew, my friends that I hung out with was smoking herb. We thought that it was the cool thing to do. We would laugh and get high as if there were no tomorrow. I guess we were in a lot of pain.

I remember we lost a teenager on Halloween night. His name was Kay. He went to someone's house who didn't want anyone knocking on his door. Kay was a smart aleck like me. When the man told Kay not to knock on his door, Kay replied, "I already did." The man pushed Kay's head through a broken elevator door, and the elevator came down and crushed his skull. My friends and

I were devastated by the tragedy. I was also frightened because this incident was even on the news. People were talking about it all through Grant Projects.

That summer, I was introduced to the biggest drug market in Harlem—123rd Street, my favorite hangout spot. Every drug you could ever want could be purchased there. I helped the Jamaicans sell their pot by telling passersby that 140th had the best chunky black on the block. At that time, I was hanging out with my friend Ness, a bad Dude who took no crap from anybody. He was my ace boom coon.

Ness and I had similar stories. We both got kicked out of Stitt Junior High School and both of our moms were alcoholics. Since Ness had been to Spofford Youth Detention Center for robbing someone, he always told me not to be scared of anyone. Together we made a few dollars here and there and smoked herb. We stayed out late and came home when we were ready. Most of the time, our moms were too drunk to even care about our whereabouts.

Ness and I laughed and snapped at people. I guess it was our way of releasing our deep pain. Eventually, Ness started hanging out with the uptown crew while I chose my homies from Grant. Although I lived in Grant Projects, I didn't hang out there too much. My Dad had moved to 111th Street right off Broadway. His place became my hangout.

I had one good friend named Artie, whom I met while hustling in the supermarket. Artie loved to hang out at my Pops' crib. He, Artie, knew for sure that we would get high and maybe even get some money. Artie's dad was a real slick dude. He used to shoot a lot of dice and chase women. I was young, but I knew his MO. He was called RoRo, the name of a dog. I wondered why RoRo was so strict with his children. He made them watch the news every day at six p.m. If I stayed with them, I too had to watch the news. I thought that was so important for us. As I look back, I commend him for some of his dictatorial ways.

Artie's dad thought that Artie and I were an awesome twosome and taught us how to be fast on our feet. Artie and my homie Jeff both lived in the Bronx, so that is where I hung out most of the time. I started hitching on the back of buses. I really thought that I was Kool Kev.

One time I was hitching on Riverside Drive with Artie and white-boy Brad, another friend. We all jumped on the side of the bus, but they quickly jumped off. I had to prove that they were suckers, so I stayed on the side of the bus. I looked up several blocks and saw a police car with its lights flashing. I got scared and jumped off while the bus was still in motion. I busted my ass and rolled down the street several yards. Artie and Brad were laughing at me when I returned limping. I still have the scar from that fall.

I never even considered my future or education; I just had fun and lived for the moment. There were no serious relationships for me, but I had started to see girls. Ma never cared for any of my girls, because she was able to see things about them that I could not.

One girl I cared for was named Charmaine. She had a beautiful face and a nice shape to go with it. She, however, was unfaithful; I busted her cheating on me with a grown man. How foolish of me to think that I was the only one tapping that. At this point in my life, I began hearing and thinking about God. My grandmother told me that if I went back to church, things might get a little better for me. She never mentioned Jesus or salvation.

Go to Church

Grandmother made this suggestion around October of '83. I decided to go to my old church, her home church, Saint John's Baptist Church. I sat in the back for two reasons: I was late, and I didn't feel appropriately dressed.

Prior to my attending church, I had read a book about the three different kinds of love: erotic love, brotherly love, and agape love, or God's love, which stuck with me the most. I was in great pain and started hearing many love songs that caused me to think about God.

This particular Sunday seemed to be the perfect day to experience God's divine plan. I don't recall the message, but the messenger was a young lady by the name of Marcy. I knew I was in the right place for the right reason. At the end of the sermon, someone gave an invitation to receive Jesus Christ as Lord and Savior. I walked from the back of the church all the way to the front. I was nervous but firm. I knew that there was something missing in my life, and I was about to say yes to whatever God wanted. I knew that He was real and my only solution.

I was led in prayer by the pastor and wept uncontrollably. God was moving in my heart, and I was truly grateful. I walked home singing a song by Alicia Myers, "I Want to Thank You." I was so happy that I forgot to buy a quart of Colt 45, my favorite beer.

I started to attend church regularly, although my bad habits were very much alive and kicking hard. I was asked to attend the Tuesday Night Bible Study, where I met one of the great women in my life, Sister Sarah Moore. She was as bold as a lion and had such an anointing on her life that I was convicted by her presence, or should I say, God's presence in her life? She taught me the true meaning of repentance. There was something about this lady that drew me to her like a magnet.

God began to truly move in my heart and teach me His love. The first Scripture I memorized was Matthew 6:33, which told me that if I focused on God's will, He would meet every one of my needs. This was to me a very profound statement of God's assurance and providence.

I was invited to the young people's Bible study. I honestly thought that the instructor was strange and gave serious thought to not attending, but I decided to give the study a shot. I'll never forget that experience. The lesson was on faith, and I left there transformed by the power of God. My initial plan after the study was to buy a beer and get some loose cigarettes, but I knew that I didn't need them any longer. God miraculously delivered me. I left there, rejoicing like never before. I was beginning to learn about my feelings.

I was excited about this supernatural experience and grew hungrier for God. I decided to join Saint John's Baptist Church's Youth Choir. I knew that I couldn't sing, but I figured that others would drown out my poor singing voice.

Sister Moore, my mentor and role model, stayed hard on my case concerning holy living. She was very generous and yet very stern with me. My new pastor, Reverend John L. Scott, was very open and available, which helped me to feel completely at home and welcome.

I must say that when I came to Saint John's Baptist Church, I brought a lot of baggage and insecurities. I was depressed and strongly addicted to many behaviors. But one thing about me is that I was always willing to work for a living. I started working at a young age. I carried groceries, sold newspapers, and even packed bags at Shopwell Supermarket just to have a few dollars in my pocket. My sister made good money packing bags and in turn taught me how to pack as well. Kim was also real good on the basketball court as I recall.

When I started attending church, I was working as a messenger, making one hundred dollars a week. I started tithing ten dollars a week because I was so grateful for God's blessings and deliverance. I knew that he would give me a better job in due season. I had such an assurance in my spirit that nothing really troubled me; I knew that God would provide for me.

My boss was okay with my drinking beer and smoking Newports, but when I got saved, things began to change drastically. We delivered boxes filled with printed materials to many locations, and I used to drink beer on every trip. All of a sudden, I didn't want to drink anymore. Instead, I was reading the Bible and listening to WWRL, a gospel station on the radio. My boss really got mad at me. Once when I was reading, my boss suggested that I give the Bible a rest. He said that I was reading too much.

I used to always share my work experiences with my pastor, who encouraged me to hang in there. Then he started talking to me about why I should go back to school and get my GED. He became a pain in my butt; he just wouldn't stop talking about my potential. I was so upset with him that I stopped going to church. I knew that if we were ever alone, he would bring up the subject of education, and I just didn't want to hear it.

As I think back, I really didn't want to get kicked out of school, but after three years of smoking dust and running from school security guards, it was time for something different. My mom didn't know what to do with me; she knew that I was definitely a troubled teenager. Prior to getting kicked out of high school, I got so many letters about me cutting classes that my mom just started sending them to my dad's house. I used to visit him every Friday to get a few dollars and a free high. Pops didn't mind my drinking and pot-smoking habits. His rationale was that as long as I got high with him, I was in a safe environment. How wrong he was.

One day, Pops called Mom's house. When I got on the phone, I knew that something was up. He suggested that I come down because he wanted to talk to me about something. My response was one that I'll never forget. I said, "You must be crazy if you think that I am stupid enough to come down." His response was that he just wanted to talk. I stayed away from him for about three weeks.

I often stayed with my friends in the Bronx for long periods of time. One Saturday, I decided to go home to Mom's. About six o'clock in the morning, I heard a loud knock on the door. With an instinct that it was Pops and nowhere to run, I was scared to death. Mom gladly let him in, and he whipped my natural behind for almost twenty minutes straight. I promised him that I would go to school. He lit up a joint and told me that he had to whip me because he wanted the best for me.

Ma had a new boyfriend named Fast Eddie. Eddie was nice to me and didn't beat Ma. I was feeling a little better. Fast Eddie got me my second real job at a place called Ducker Printing. I was a bike messenger for two dollars and fifty cents an hour. I was thrilled. I drank a lot of alcohol and was often fired and rehired. My drinking increased because I now had a steady income.

My good friend, whom I called Jeff to the Left, needed a job. I hooked him up with a job where I worked, and he was promoted over me. I couldn't believe it. Jeff was a better worker than me, and he didn't drink on the job. After several drinking binges and being late to work several times, I was fired. But I didn't care, because I was hired by a truck messenger named Harvey Harris. I thought Harris was so cool because he let me drink during almost every truck delivery.

Harvey was a sucker. He used me because I was a good worker. He paid me a hundred a week and probably got close to a thousand a week. I worked my butt off for him. He would lend me about five dollars a day to support my habit. By the end of the week, all I had was seventy-five dollars. Sixty went to rent, so I always managed to stay broke.

Although Harvey cheated me and used me as slave labor, he really helped me stay out of criminal activity. He was to me what you might call a godsend. I worked with Harvey for about three years, and it was really not that bad.

My drinking continued to progress. I drank morning, noon, and night. While others ordered coffee to start their day, I ordered a quart of Colt 45 malt liquor. I was about to be nineteen years old and was extremely unhappy with my life.

chapter 3
WHAT'S THE POINT?

Before I began attending church my dad told me that he could get me a job making more money than I ever made before. I was about 19 years old. Dad knew that I was a hard worker and that, even though he didn't raise me, I had learned to work and hustle at a very young age. I carried groceries for people when I was eight and always sold newspapers.

I started working in August at three in the morning, unloading a freight car loaded with potatoes and oranges. It was hard work. I will never forget the conversation I had with myself. I said, "Kevin, if you can make it through the night, you will surely get paid."

We stopped at about seven for lunch, and Pops took me to Helen's Diner. We got fish, egg,s and grits. I was so tired that I could barely eat. Pops laughed with Helen about how I stalled because I didn't want to go back to the potato car. Man, I was tired. We went back and finished unloading the freight cars, and I got paid fifty dollars. I was so happy that I made so much money in one day.

Two weeks later, Pops went on vacation and they paid me his exact salary. Every Friday, I walked away with $386!

The more money I made, the more I drank. I had no idea that I had a drinking problem. It was at the market that I learned how to drink half a pint of Smirnoff and chase it with a can of Budweiser. I learned how to work while on heroin and cocaine at the same time. I stole from my job. Alcohol and drugs really affected my life. I was a complete mess. I started to show up for work late. I called in sick. I really was in a great deal of pain.

One thing stands out around that time. My number-one hobby was riding bikes. I had stolen many bikes in my younger years, but I purchased a brand-new, red, twenty-eight-inch Panasonic ten-speed bike. I would never lend it out and barely allowed anyone to ride it. One time, I had to go to work and my brother asked if he could borrow my bike. I reluctantly lent it to him. It was a Friday, pay day. I was so happy to have so much money, plus I was fly. I had all of the Adidas and Puma shoes I wanted.

You see, I don't know about you, but I grew up with hand-me-downs. Kenny used to take my money and some of the nice things I had, too. I came home from working very hard that day, and Kenny told me that someone had stolen my bike. I was devastated and angry as hell. That was the day I truly became a man. I was going to break Kenny's jaw! This was the first time that he had ever backed down from me.

Kenny never bothered me again. He never put his hands on me or talked crap to me again. He knew that I was serious.

I was so upset that I got pissy drunk. I continued to work and slowly die.

The Transformation

About the same time, I started dating this young lady by the name of Mae Mae. She wasn't the finest chick in the world, but she sure had a big butt. I spent a lot of my money on her, and she loved it. We would break up and then make up with some real good sex. I was a very careless and depressed young man.

I always needed someone to validate me. Mae Mae had a brother who became and still is one of the best friends I ever had. His name was John, but we called him Artie. He was always bailing me out of trouble. I drank too much, so I never remembered most of the crap that I did under the influence. I talked a lot of junk to people I didn't even know.

I recall when Artie and I had gone to see *Caveman*. I was so high and drunk that when a police cruiser drove by while we were smoking a joint, I told Artie that since I was from Harlem, I could smoke right in front of the police. When they saw us, they asked me to come to the car. I was scared to death. All of a sudden, I was no longer high. Eventually, they told me to get the hell home and that they better not catch me over there again. We still laugh about it to this day.

Artie and I worked in a supermarket, carrying groceries for people. We made good money and often went to see karate movies on Sundays. I had no idea that his father was a slickster, a street term for a con man and a convicted rapist. I had a great deal of respect for his dad even though I found out that he had attempted to rape my own mother. I didn't know how to handle the situation. I wanted to fight Artie, but he didn't do it. His father was the one who conned me into giving him my phone number.

When I look back, there were so many things that really troubled me, and I didn't have a clue as to how to relieve the pain. I'll discuss this more in another chapter.

One day while working in the market, I was asked if I would be willing to do a double shift. The first thing that came to mind was the extra money that I would make. I had no idea of what I was in for. My work hours were from eight a.m. until four p.m., with no lunch period, and then from four p.m. until midnight.

I remember it as if it were yesterday. I began thinking about the value of the many produce crates that I was watching. I told myself that the hours between five and ten p.m. would be hell. I sat in the front of the store on a gray stool, thinking about the possibility of someone trying to steal something. How would I defend myself? All of a sudden, this fear that I can't explain washed over me. At that very moment, I felt a sense of supernatural power that I cannot describe.

For the first time in my life, I experienced God's presence. God had come into one of the most sinful areas in New York and showed me that He is indeed a present help in the time of trouble. The only thing that I could say was, "Lord, what do you want me to do?" He didn't speak audibly, but to my heart, He said, "Do My will, My way." I kept saying, "Yes, Lord" for about an hour. I was so overcome with joy that at once the fear left me. It wasn't hell at all, but truly heaven on Earth. That was the greatest experience of my life and the first of many others.

The following Sunday morning, I went to Saint John's Baptist Church and surrendered my life to Christ. For the first time in my life, I felt the true peace of God that passes all human understanding. My life was changed.

There was another young man who felt the same tug of God at the same time, who also surrendered his life to Christ and today pastors a church in the heart of Harlem.

I started attending a new members class and met the teacher, Evangelist Sarah Moore, who became my spiritual mother. She deposited much of her Christian faith into my spirit and ministered to me in such a unique way. As I attended Bible study, the Word transformed my life and enhanced my walk with God.

I got fired at that job and left the market for about a month. When I returned, I was a born-again Christian. I got a job at E. Arnata Produce and worked the day shift for a while and then switched to nights. My co-workers knew my dad and were very helpful in showing me the ropes. That company was larger so it had a wide variety of produce. I worked very hard, and all the employees had a mandatory overtime obligation.

This is where I met one of my best friends, Stan the Man. We always walked to the subway together, became close, and worked well together. I watched Stan save his money and purchase his first house. Within six months I was promoted to the front door checker position. It was not the foreman position, but I had authority over some other workers and received a raise of one hundred dollar a week.

My new position was very stressful, but I managed to stay away from drugs and alcohol. I was truly serving God, and he blessed all that my hands touched. My employees showed me the greatest respect and were very kind to me.

One in Every Bunch

The three owners of E. Armata each had two sons working in the market. When the three fathers turned over responsibility to their sons, all hell broke loose. They did not cooperate with each other. I really worked well with two of them, but one was my worst nightmare. He knew that I was a Christian and gave me a very hard time, and I was always tired and upset by the time I arrived home from work. I threatened to resign from the position, but this guy never stopped harassing me. He seemed to find pleasure in annoying me. After eight years of quality service and much time spent in prayer, I resigned. I took a one-week vacation and never looked back.

I didn't go far. I received a job offer right next door at my old job and took the position one week later. The cut in my salary was frightening to say the least, but I was very happy. I stayed at that company for seven years and was there when I received my opportunity to go back to school. The Hunts Point Market has really been good to me and for me.

What Happens when You Serve God?

The Bible states that if you seek first the kingdom of God, he will meet your every need.Matthew 6:33 KJV This was the first Scripture that I learned and memorized. I had enough sense to apply this Scripture to my life. I'm amazed at how God began to move in my life and on my behalf. I watched as God met my every need and gave me many extra blessings.

I was hungry for the presence of God. I prayed and fasted almost daily. My heart overflowed with the joy of the Lord as I began to understand holy things. God put people in my life who truly nourished my spirit. My pastor was my greatest influence. He became my spiritual father and really poured himself into me. Of course, there was the other person whom God used to minister to me, which was my spiritual mom, Evangelist Sarah Moore.

chapter 4

AFFLICTION BY ADDICTION

If only I knew that stealing and drinking that cup of vodka would take me places that I never wanted to go, perhaps I never would have stolen it.

By the age of twelve, I had watched Ma drink so much, get beat up, and get drunk again, day after depressing day. So I got the bright idea that if I drank some of her vodka, maybe it would stop her from getting drunk again—that if I drank it, she wouldn't have any to drink. That bright idea started a vicious cycle in my life that I would repeat for years, but at that time, I had no clue.

Afflict means to cause pain or extreme suffering. Addiction is a very bad habit that is almost never broken. To combine affliction with addiction can only mean utter disaster and destruction. To think that I did this to myself is very frightening to say the least.

I started early and suffered for many, many years. I also caused a great deal of pain to those around me, especially those I truly loved. I will never forget the first drink out of that green cup. It didn't take long until I was drunk and feeling real good. My depression was gone, and I could say everything that I felt and anything that I wanted to say. I was bold, careless, and just didn't give a damn! I was free, or so I thought. In reality, I was locked, loaded, set up for one of the greatest deceptions in life.

Alcohol opened up a can of worms. It had the power to change me and my behavior. I had blackouts, lost jobs, and even got arrested several times. You couldn't tell me anything. I was the man. Just give me a drink, and I was good. I even broke Ma's TV.

I disrespected my best friend Artie's mother and then forgot all about it. When he reminded me, I felt bad. Alcohol was my best friend. It helped me talk to girls; like I said, it made me bold. But hangovers were part of the package that I really didn't care for. I had some of the worst hangovers that one could possibly imagine.

Colt 45 was one of my choice drinks. I loved beer. I used to take a long ride on the bus to Artie's in the Castle Hill House. I would buy one quart and one tall can of beer for the ride. By the time I arrived, I was drunk. Artie is still the best friend I have ever had. He never saw me as the drunk that I had become. He saw me as the godly man I am today. What a friend!

My drinking only got worse. I was very rude to many. If I was not drunk or drinking, I was very depressed and sad. I honestly thought that I needed alcohol to survive. Although I watched many people suffer and die, I had no desire to stop. I was hooked.

I started working early in life, so I always had the money to support my habit. I was on a suicide mission and didn't even realize it. Then I started drinking with Ma. Imagine a teenaged boy drinking vodka with his mother. What insanity! I started playing numbers because that is what she did. We played cards, drank, and acted foolishly. It wasn't until many years later that I realized that Ma was very depressed also.

Where was my dad? He was living twelve blocks away, smoking weed and drinking Heineken. Pops kept a job but was insatiable when it came to drinking and drugging. I used to think he wrote the book on it. He too would drink with me and my siblings. My crew thought my dad was the man. They really enjoyed his one-room studio apartment with the bathroom in the hallway. Pops was also a damned good cook, which alone drew a lot of family and friends. The truth was that anyone who came into his apartment was using or selling something.

My favorite time was the weekend. Dad got paid on Friday and was always drunk by the time he arrived home. He would turn the music up loud and we danced, drank, and smoked weed. But he was abusive to his women. He even broke one lady's jaw. I vowed to never to hit women as long as I lived.

Hanging with Pops, I learned a great deal of bad habits, one of them being how to do a shotgun with a joint: You hold the joint in your mouth and blow the smoke out the other end.

I met a white boy named Brad who lived in Pops' building, which had a lot of strange characters. Two strange people happened to be Brad's parents.

Brad became my best friend. We smoked a lot of angel dust. There were brand names for the dust we smoked like Red Devil, Two-Puff Dust, and Triple X. The slogan at that time was, "Dust is a must."

The dust epidemic resulted in a lot of people in Grant Projects jumping out of windows and run down the street naked. It still didn't stop me—remember, I was da man. Sure I was. I was da man outta control with no sense of direction.

I always told Brad to wait for me before going to cop dust. One day, he had a bright idea to surprise me. The dust was in Harlem; it was the seventies, and Brad was white with blond hair and blue eyes. I don't know what he was thinking. Guess what happened? He got robbed and had to run for his life through the Lenox Avenue subway tunnel.

Brad loved Pops as well. He spent a great deal of time at Pop's house. He too was trying to escape his own home. You guessed it—his mom was being physically abused in the worse way and often by her black guy named Ben. He kept giving her black eyes, and she always wore sunglasses.

I really cared for Brad, he was like a brother. We laughed so much together and also used a lot of drugs.

Although Mom and Dad were heavily addicted to drugs and alcohol, they experienced the marvelous power of God through recovery at Alcoholics Anonymous. Ma went first. She went to meetings on a regular basis and got very involved with the process called recovery. I don't think that she ever relapsed. She then gave her heart to Jesus and honestly lived happily ever after.

Ma was very happy and serious about serving God. She enrolled in the Manhattan Bible Institute and scored above a ninety average in almost all of her exams. She was hungry for more of Jesus. What a true miracle she was! Ma was a giver and a lover of life, and she cherished her grandchildren. She spoiled them every chance she got. My Shannel and Kevin, Jr. loved Ma and the cute cartoon cups she bought them.

What a Sign!

How unfortunate that Ma would succumb to her zodiac sign of Cancer. She was truly a fighter. She was first diagnosed with cancer in 1991, just after having open heart surgery for the fourth time. But it didn't stop her from attending Borough of Manhattan Community College, though, where she obtained an Associate's Degree in Mental Health. She met a special schoolmate from Spain and dreamed of traveling there but never made it. Maybe one of her grandchildren will one day take the trip in dedication to her.

Ma suffered very long. It was unbearable to watch. She became helpless but maintained her strong faith in God. She was so serious about her recovery that she called her sponsor concerning the medication she was given. She didn't want to take it. She remembered the affliction by addiction.

After a long relentless battle, Ma went home to be with the Lord on September 26, 1996. She was a super trooper. I know that if I continue to serve God, I will see her again and in a better place. I have no doubt that she will be there.

Utter Desperation

Pops and I didn't really talk too much unless there was some sort of drug involvement. He did, however, tell me his story after several years of his being in recovery. Prior to that, I held a great deal of resentment against him. I thought that I had forgiven him, but I had no idea how deep it was until I opened myself up in counseling. I am so grateful that there are professionals who can really help in the process called healing. I always thought that if you needed help, you were crazy. How fool I was. Counseling really helped me to uncover and discover in order to recover.

Pops told me about the last day he used drugs. He wanted to kill himself. Just before he stepped onto the Bruckner Boulevard Expressway, he saw a man with no legs, begging for change, and that startled him. All that he had in his pocket was the information Ma had given him to a treatment center.

Pops walked all the way from the Bronx to 114th Street and Amsterdam Avenue, utterly desperate, to the treatment center. He was admitted and thus began his process called recovery. Although he held onto his job at the Bronx Terminal Market, he had several relapses. Today, however, he celebrates over twenty years clean. Imagine that! I honestly thought that Pops would die from addictions.

He had many blackouts and seizures on the job. They always called me, and I had to leave my job and meet him at any given hospital. One time was right after I had paid off a $2,500 loan that he had reneged on. I was truly pissed off. I just couldn't let it go even though I thought that I had. I didn't know how to forgive. My scars were deeply rooted.

Not until I met with a good friend who was into Christian counseling was God able to open my eyes to the legacy of Mom's and Dad's recovery, which was mine for the taking. He encouraged me to go into counseling because I saw my parents recover so well. My recovery has been a long bumpy ride, filled with relapses due to my unwillingness to completely surrender. Today, I thank God for Narcotics Anonymous and Alcoholics Anonymous. I needed them both then and still need them today.

Although I started attending AA and NA meetings in 1996 as I was about to lose Ma, I didn't really open up to the recovery process until July 2005. God really planned it well.

In 2003, I had lost what was to me the greatest job that I ever had—other than serving God, which was teaching—due to my strong addiction to cocaine. I just could not stop using. I had snorted coke in my early years, but there was something different about it this time. Coke made me a prisoner and held me captive for years. It was a bondage that I wouldn't wish on my worst enemy. I missed weddings, funerals, preaching engagements, and caused many people a great deal of pain. I rejected my own children and almost caused the death of my grandmother when she heard that I was arrested for purchasing drugs. What a disgrace! Although it was one of my greatest learning experiences, I still didn't stop.

When I was arrested, my family, my friends, colleagues, church members deserted me and treated me like pure crap, even the so-called church. There was, however, my good friend and my son. They were all I had. I was crushed and continuously stepped on like dirt. I hold no resentments, but I'll never forget that experience. It taught me a lot. I had to go away for treatment. But I went because everyone knew what had taken place; I wasn't really seeking recovery.

On day twenty-seven in treatment, I got kicked out because I was rude to a nurse. I stayed clean for thirty-five days before I was back to the races. I had no job and, although I faithfully paid my tithes, the church offered very little assistance. I felt that they really didn't know how to exemplify the true love and mercy of Christ. I was angry and hurt. I later realized that they just didn't know how to minister to a fallen soldier who had embarrassed them. My friend and my son really held me down.

I knew that I could get work at the Point Market, but I was too ashamed, so I applied for welfare and was denied. Eight months later, I went back to the market and was hired instantly because they knew me and trusted my past experience. The market, however, is one of the biggest drugstores in the South Bronx, and I started using very heavily again.

One week in particular, I stayed up for three days straight. I worked, went to a hotel, and sniffed coke. There were no hookers to cheat me out of money; it was just porno movies, coke, and me.

I was good money, or so I thought! Before long, the drugs turned me into a monster. I was in much pain, so I caused pain. I was supposed to preach for my cousin in Staten Island, but I never made that service. The coke really whipped me good.

Two years later, even though I was still using, my best friend Artie was graduating from a program. He told me that no one was coming. I had to show up for him because he is my best friend. I had just planned to support him, nothing more. But God had other plans.

The speaker was a guy I'll call P.W. As soon as he spoke, I was convicted of how I had mistreated my wife. I cried throughout the whole service. It got so good that it didn't matter who was looking. I had already changed my seat from the front to the back so that I could cry freely.

That day was the first time that I honestly opened up to the process called recovery. I even cried on the way home. I took notes so that I could remember to respect my wife and treat her better.

I didn't make meetings, and once again, I was back in that lonely room with no more coke or money, just dying for another hit. Several weeks later, I was stuck at a hotel way over in the east Bronx. I had spent the whole day there and had to be at work at ten p.m. I called my good alcoholic friend Stan to share my predicament. I couldn't drive, because I was too paranoid.

Stan and a girlfriend came to get me. She drove his car, and he drove my car. I expected him to stop for a beer. I just knew that he would, but he didn't stop at all. He told me that he had stopped drinking and had recently gone away for treatment. What a surprise! Here was the guy I had started drinking with in the first place, and now he was sober. He also told me something that I hope to never forget. As he exited my car and handed me my keys, he said, "Yo, Kev, you can start your day over at any given time." That sticks with me to this very day.

I was jealous that he had gotten clean before me but happy that he had given me so much hope that night. I made it through the night at work and got high again the next day. But the seed had been planted at Artie's graduation and watered by Stan's kind words of hope. I realized that I had a shot at it.

In early July, I used again, but this time, I did something different: I surrendered totally to any help that I could get. I called Stan, and he gave me information to a treatment center just like Ma gave to Pops. I followed through, but my wife really didn't think anything about this promise. She just wanted me out of the house. So out I went.

The arrangements were made for my stay at a place where I would get help. Clearbrook Rehab picked me up early in the morning, and I cried all the way to Pennsylvania. That journey deserves a book of its own. It took a while for me to get adjusted, and they allowed me five days of complete rest. I took advantage of it.

Soon, I changed my seat from the back of the lecture to the front row. The back section was called "denial aisle." I did a great deal of weeping as I began to take an honest look at myself. That is one of the hardest things for one to really do. It takes honesty and open-mindedness along with willingness to change the horrible addictive behaviors.

The time in the treatment center proved to be one of my greatest life experiences. I met lawyers, doctors, and people of all cultures and backgrounds who had a common problem: addiction. We all ate, laughed, cried, and recovered together. I heard stories from people who suffered great losses due to this disease that takes no prisoners and doesn't care about what you have or whom you know. Addiction is deadly and moves cunningly from generation to generation. Addiction is bondage sent directly from the Devil to kill, steal, and destroy. Satan has been around for a long time and has caused many disasters by means of addiction.

Many addicts were just like me. They knew no way out and died from their addiction. One of the prayers spoken by recovering addicts is for those who are about to use or drink for the first time. They have no idea what they're about to encounter. They are unaware of the invisible handcuffs that appear without a key. It all seems like fun in the beginning, but there is always hell to pay. It seems appealing. Some people are able to take a hit or a drink and never use again until they choose to.

I know many people who are social drinkers, weed smokers, and coke users. I also know and have heard many stories regarding the horrors of active addiction. I am very, very grateful for God's amazing grace that led me and many others to the process called recovery.

My first sponsor and true friend is Yum Yum. He always states before he speaks or shares at a meeting, "I did not earn this seat in recovery. It's only through God's grace and mercy that I'm here." Yum Yum used to sleep on the streets, made friends with rats, and drank rubbing alcohol. He is now a shining example of God's power to heal. Yum Yum is always ready and willing to help someone. He truly helped me.

I know a guy, whose name I won't mention, who is still suffering. He has been addicted for well over forty years. Can you imagine that kind of suffering? No, you can't unless you've been there. He's angry, bitter, and in a lot of pain, but that's not the worse part. He is in denial and viciously hurting all those within his circle of insane madness. It troubles me so much as this is someone I truly love and respect. When you've been on both sides, you really empathize with the suffering person. Sometimes we fail to recognize and realize the damage that our behavior causes others. They are often left scarred and will often repeat the cycle of addiction. If we only knew better, maybe we'd break the deadly repetition.

Just for today, I will be grateful and focus on my journey of recovery. I will look for opportunities to assist those in the struggle. I will share my experience, strength, and hope. I must remember from whence I've come. I won't allow situations and life's storms to fool me into believing that I can use just one more time. I have to stay connected to those who have been where I've been. Their stories keep me going, but my story keeps me clean, just for today.

chapter 5
MERCY, MERCY ME

The word *mercy* means considerable kindness and pity. Something that is not deserved and cannot be purchased. Mercy is synonymous with grace.

I worked with a guy named Harvey Harris. Harris is someone whom I'll always be grateful to. He hired me when I got fired from Ducker Printing for drinking too much on the job. Harris knew that I had this problem and still hired me. He knew that I was damned good worker. He drove a big green van and needed assistance transporting boxes of printed material. I really don't wish to focus on Harris but more on what God did.

We would deliver about twenty to thirty boxes to Westchester, New York, to a place called Mercy College. I loved that trip because I could get a quart of beer for the ride which was a nice long ride. It was also our last trip for the day, which made it even more enjoyable.

Mercy College was a big campus. I never thought about school after getting kicked out of Martin Luther King High School because I was eighteen years old and had absolutely no credits. I never went to class or took any exams. I just didn't try.

After leaving Harris for a much better job at Hunts Point Terminal Market, about eight to ten years later, I went back to Mercy College for a graduation of a friend's sister. It was the year that the Mets won the World Series because Mookie Wilson, the Mets player also graduated from Mercy College. Jerry Lewis received an honorary degree, and I believe he was the keynote speaker. Anyway, it was my second encounter with that great institution of higher learning. On that particular occasion, I actually thought about the possibility of one day sitting where those graduating students sat. It was a real serious thought that didn't last too long. I continued to work at the market, and the money was real good. I was happy and had been converted, so I felt that I was okay.

I often fought with my pastor, Reverend Scott, over returning to school to obtain my GED. I was very adamant about not returning. I had failed the test once by twenty-six points. I thought I had passed, so I finally enrolled in an education program to prepare for it again. This time I failed by only nine points. Although I was discouraged, I was very happy with such an improvement. I was done, though, and didn't want to hear about school or any test anymore. But Reverend Scott was very persistent. I now know that he saw something in me that I could not see in myself. I loved, honored, and respected him then and still do now.

In 1995, Mercy College came to the Hunts Point Terminal Market to offer courses to any employee who wanted to (get this) obtain a GED while earning college credit. I could not believe it!

I had recently attended a church service and was called out by the man of God, who spoke The Word over my life. Then he told me something that really offended me: that God would have me working with college students. I was furious. How could this servant of God speak this over my life? How could he speak so accurately and seemingly miss God.

When I saw the Mercy College poster in the market, I knew that I had to obey. I knew that it was of God. The union paid some money toward my tuition, which was reduced, and my employer also paid a portion. How could I not take advantage of such a golden opportunity? Only seven of us workers out of 1,500 in the market registered. We called ourselves the Magnificent Seven.

The classes were every Saturday at the market from nine a.m. to three p.m. I loved it. Our first courses were The College Experience and Psych 119. The book was one of the best books that I have ever read. I still have a copy. That book, to me, is the bible of education as it covered everything that I needed to know about how to excel in college. Wow! I was engaging my mind with others, learning from them and about them. I was hooked on learning. I needed twenty-four credits to earn a GED.

I now had a short-term goal, and Ma was about as excited as me. She was very encouraging and even went with me to several events for particular assignments. We went to an opera together and also attended the museum while I studied evolution.

Upon completion of those classes, we had a ceremony, and I was chosen to speak for the class. In my speech, I recited a poem that I had written.

Those first two classes were very enticing and rewarding, but they were soon over, and I was left with the question, Should I continue? There would be no discount for tuition any longer, and I really would feel the fifty dollars that would be taken out of my check each week.

I struggled with the decision and discovered that none of the other guys were going to continue, which made my struggle even harder. But you never know where your encouragement is going to come from. I was very surprised when my employer, who was a white lady, told me that I should continue. I always believed that white people thought that they were better than blacks and did not want black people to succeed. I was wrong, dead wrong.

Mama Lee, another church mother, as I called her, was also encouraging to me, which I will never ever forget it. She assured me that the money that I would have to pay would not measure or compare to the education that I would receive if I only persevered. I had received Bs in the two classes I had taken and had learned so much. I was ready to learn more. In the fall semester, I registered.

I was really terrified in my first course on campus, which was English 109. But I had a good professor—so good that I took two more English classes with him. In each class, I obtained an A, which inspired me to work even harder and to stay focused.

I remember walking down the hall and seeing some of the student's names on a board called the Dean's List of Scholars. I saw my first dean one day and asked her how one got on that list. She told me that a student had to earn a 3.7 grade point average or better. I now had a new goal.

By the end of the next semester, I was on that wall, and the school had a ceremony for us. That is where I met my good friend Rodd. We were the only black males at the function, and we became friends quickly. We encouraged each other. Little did I know that we would become adjunct professors for our school, Mercy College.

Rod went on to obtain his PhD, and we lost contact, but I'll always remember him. He was such a blessing to my life.

I could tell you about many others whom I met at Mercy College who have a very big place in my heart. The librarian was a sweet lady named Brenda. She was always very helpful to all students and was like a big sister to me. She really inspired me to read more books than I ever dreamed. I soon got involved with the Student Government Organization and was elected vice president.

The president of SGO was a very intelligent, articulate, drop-dead gorgeous lady named Glynis. By this time, I had separated from my first wife, and Glynis and I started dating. She was one of the best friends and sweethearts that I ever had.

I must be honest; when I first met Glynis, I was very intimidated by her persona. When she walked into any room, she attracted all attention to herself without any effort. She was very smart and yet very humble. I still have much love for Glynis. We are still good friends, and she's doing quite well for herself.

Mercy College had talent shows, where I once won second prize for my poetry. We also took several all-expense paid trips to the Black Student Leadership Conference. I was so inspired by some of the greatest motivational speakers that I've ever heard. It was a good learning experience for me.

Rusty, another person whom I met at Mercy College, was a real character. Russ, as I called him, used to like to drink a lot. Maybe even a little too much. I thought that I was cool back in the days when I rode the bus to Artie's house with a quart and a tall can of beer. But Russ used to bring a forty-ounce bottle of beer to school and sat in the lounge and drank it! Then he would steal a sandwich from the school cafeteria. The owner would call me to the side and say, "Your friend just stole a sandwich." I'd pay for the food and get on Russ' case, but he didn't care at all.

Russ came drunk to class many times. We started riding home together because we had a late class, and before long, I was drinking Heinekens with him. We now had something in common, and our friendship grew stronger. I could go home and fall right to sleep from the beer, which soon proved to be an addictive sedative that affected my work and school performance.

I was depressed over my failed marriage. My ex-wife would come to the school dressed in ways that distracted me and only increased my pain. And my mom's health was getting worse. People at the school saw my pain and were very supportive and encouraging, but I still ran back to my best friend, cocaine. What a mess! I almost flunked out, but I didn't. Only God's mercy kept me in Mercy College.

In 1994, I was arrested and charged with attempted assault. I said that I would never hit a female, but alcohol had other plans. I'll never forget that night, because my son, who was six or seven at the time, witnessed the whole event. It was tragic. The arrest didn't happen immediately, so I really suffered and was overwhelmed with fear. Eventually, I turned myself in and had to go through the system, an absolutely frightening experience to say the least.

All that I remember about the incident is that this girl from school pushed me and I punched her. I was so drunk that my ex-wife was the only one who could persuade me to go upstairs after the occurrence. Both the girl and I felt very uncomfortable at school, and I'm sure that many others heard the story. But I managed to stay in school and get my GED and associates degree.

Ma was fading fast, and my Aunt and my Grandmother suggested that I take a semester off. I spoke to Ma about it, but she said, "No matter what happens, please don't stop." My family was very upset, but I stayed in school. I even went to class on the day of the funeral. My mom was always there for me when it came to school. I miss her deeply.

As I began to prepare for graduation, the librarian asked me which master's program I was considering. Around that time, I was taking a course called Statistics for Social and Behavioral Science. All I wanted was to get through that course. I almost dropped the class, but a fellow student encouraged me to hang in there.

But the librarian would not stop with this master's stuff. One day, she asked me to drop her off somewhere and started talking about how well I'd do in a master's program. About halfway to her destination, I told her that if she said another word about it that I would pull over and put her out of the car. She still pursued the issue until she arrived safely at her destination.

Around the same time, the school offered a master's program in the field of Organizational Leadership. The program was a one-year master's degree broken up into four modules. I was instantly attracted and started the registration almost immediately. I also needed to complete summer courses in order to have the necessary 120 credits. I loved Mercy College because it opened many new experiences for me, and I learned so much.

In September, I started the master's program. By now, school had become easy for me. I started my papers as soon as they were assigned, which to me was a key to succeeding in college. The lectures were fun because I always contributed or asked questions that led to a big discussion on any given subject. Ethics in Leadership was a great class. We had many great, informative talks that related to current events.

At that time, pornography on the Internet was a big subject. I wrote a paper on it and got an A. The professor suggested that all students in the program attend a job fair that was hosted at Jimmy's Café, where one of my classmates challenged me to a drinking contest. He must have weighed three hundred pounds, easy. To top that off, he said we could only drink 151-proof rum. All I remember is all the vomit I left in his car and that he rarely spoke to me for the rest of the semester.

I was still very active in Mercy's student government programs and helped a lot of freshmen students. I was asked to give a seminar and was paid almost three hundred dollars. My education at Mercy College was already beginning to pay off.

That one drunken stupor also benefited me. I overslept and was immediately fired. My supervisor was very upset at my attending school. I would show him my papers before I handed them in, and he would say, "Maybe you'll get a C." Then I'd bring that same paper back with an A. He was really out to fire me. However, his mother would hang my graded papers up all around the warehouse, which only infuriated him. When I called him, he told me that I was fired. He was wrong because I was late only once that year. My union rep told me to collect unemployment and continue with my education. He assured me that if I wanted to return to the market that he would guarantee my employment. My employers, union, and myself all agreed that I would be laid off, not terminated. I collected unemployment and still unloaded trailers at the market. My supervisor was angry with me to say the least. The sad part for me was Mama Leona, one of my employers was upset too.

At Mercy, I met many people. I knew all of the security guards and maintenance personnel. They wouldn't clip my lock, so I kept the same locker for years. We had a small weight room at the campus, so I started working out.

The Bronx campus was a very small building and parking was very hectic. I had just purchased a Cadillac Cimarron that had only twelve thousand miles on it. What a deal! I knew how to beat the crowd by arriving early, so I had very little parking problems.

There were only about ten students in my class, and we really got a chance to know each other. We worked hard and had a lot of fun together. The professors were knowledgeable in their areas of concentration, which really caused me to hunger for more of their wisdom.

Professor McFinney was a real piece of work. Everyone told me not to take her course, but I was very stubborn. She taught a science class called Plants and People, which sounded simple, but boy, was I in for a surprise. That was one of the hardest courses that I ever took, and I failed. I chased Professor McFinney around all summer. I had to do some extra work, but I would not give up and finally settled for a D. Let that be a lesson—failure is not final.

I also took an easy computer class. I thought that the professor was funny, so I made fun of him. He failed me too. The grade never changed, but I wrote these words:

"I'm Glad I Failed that Class"

I'm glad I failed that class in spite of so much pain.
The second time around an A I will obtain.
The reason for this failure, as I do contemplate,
I really didn't focus or concentrate.
The student that I am was hidden in a cage
And when I saw the F I vented so much rage.

53

The second time around, I'll do more than just pass
But as I think about it now,
I'm glad I failed that class.

Those failing experiences were all part of my process at Mercy College. They taught me a lot. I was at Mercy College for a total of eight years, and in that time, I obtained my GED, my associate's degree, and my bachelor's degree in psychology. I also earned a master's degree in organizational leadership and a master's in elementary education. I am six credits away from my third master's degree, this one in supervision and administration in education and have received my Administrative and Supervisory Certification. I have achieved all that I have only through God's mercy. It's never been mercy, mercy me but rather God's mercy for me.

chapter 6
DON'T GET MARRIED
UNTIL ...

People marry for different reasons. Some marry out of pure love for each other. Many marry simply because a baby is coming, believing that marriage is the right thing to do. I've even told someone to marry because of pregnancy, but I was wrong. People also marry for financial reasons.. Marriage is a sacred act between a man and a woman.

I could not write my life story, hoping to inspire others, without discussing the subject of marriage. I definitely am not the expert on this matter, but my experiences can guarantee that you'll do better in marriage than I did if you'll consider these words of wisdom.

My first marriage was a real disaster, and I have no one to blame but myself. I was young and ignorant as to what it means to commit your life to someone, to be absolutely honest, patient, and faithful. I married for the wrong reasons and suffered severely. I was very selfish and knew little about sharing and caring for a woman. I make no excuses for my failed marriage and recognize that some may be offended, but this is my story. I must tell it as it occurred.

I had lived alone for a period of time and practiced celibacy for six months. I was very hot and wanted a companion. I wanted to be married. I knew that I could not sleep around anymore because I had surrendered my life to Christ. I wanted sex bad, but I never considered truly loving someone and being a responsible husband. I could say that I married for sex.

There were other selfish reasons that I wanted to get married. I wanted to look upstanding. I wanted a female friend because at that point in my life I had none. Any decent young lady who came close to me I wanted to screw. Friendship with a female was foreign to me; I didn't realize that two people of the opposite sex could be friends without ulterior motives for sex. I have, however, since learned the true value of having female friends who are friends or sisters in Christ.

My soon-to-be wife was very attractive—what I would call dark and lovely—and had a good head on her shoulders. She cooked like a chef and wasn't a fast woman. We dated for a short time before we had sex, and now I realize that was a big mistake. She didn't get pregnant, but the sexual encounter created a bond that drew me closer to her quicker than normal. I always felt bad after the sex but never during or before.

At that time, I had a spiritual mother with whom I shared everything. I believed everything that she said because she was serious about serving God. She told me to either stop having sex or get married. No sex to me was out of the question, so we quickly became engaged and got married. What a big mistake. I didn't realize it then, but I had headed down the wrong road. We had received no counseling at all. I didn't really even discuss getting married with my pastor. I guess I knew that he would have suggested counseling.

We got married at city hall. That in itself was very uncomfortable for me. Deep down inside I knew better. She had lived at home with her mother and other siblings, and I had been living in a decent, one-bedroom apartment. When we got married, she moved in and changed the whole house. I was angry but afraid to share my anger with her because I didn't want to hurt her feelings.

I had learned the very bad habit of people pleasing. I later learned that when one is a people-pleaser, he or she will always suffer pain while the other is okay or even happy. I kept a lot of things bottled up and was sure to explode. And boy did I.

I knew that my wife really loved me, which she showed by her actions. She was very supportive and knew how to minister to my needs. The problem was that our relationship was all about my needs and not hers. I really didn't know how to be a husband, lover, or friend, so I didn't try. I worked very hard and long hours, so I didn't spend any quality time with her except during sex. Even that was all about me.

When I look back on that marriage, I have many regrets. I took her for granted and expected much from her, while giving little or nothing in return. I still had a heart full of lust, the exact opposite of love. Lust desires to please itself at the expense of others because lust desires to receive. Love, on the other hand, wants to please others at the expense of self because love desires to give. My wife gave and gave, and I took and took. She shared; I hoarded.

She soon saw me for the person I was. I cheated on her and told her. I was out of control. Whenever I didn't get my way, I became verbally abusive. She always asked me if I wanted to have children, and I said no. I honestly did not want to raise children in such rough times in society, so I thought. I think that unconsciously I didn't want to lose any of her affection or undivided attention. She already had a daughter. Although I kept saying no to children, somehow my heart changed on the matter. Several days later, my wife tearfully asked me again, and I said I would like to have children. She then told me that she was several weeks pregnant, and I was delighted. Only God could have done changed my heart like that. Only God.

But I was still the same selfish guy. One night, around the time that I was getting ready to head to work, she got sick and wanted me to go with her to the hospital. I actually thought work was more important until she phoned Reverend Scott, who almost had to make me go with to the hospital. I didn't realize how much my being with her meant to her. She was afraid, and I was careless and clueless.

What I Saw

The marriages and relationships I witnessed were all dysfunctional. They consisted of abusive or absent husbands and abused wives on welfare. From childhood to adulthood, I saw selfishness, anger, bitterness, and total chaos.

Ma had friends who were married. Bill and Mary drank and fought just about every time that we visited them. Mary was more violent and she caused more damage. We spent a lot of time there, so we witnessed much violence. I wish that someone would have advised me about how to really treat a lady.

My first marriage dissolved very rapidly. There was infidelity on both sides. e parties and loved the . One day, I walked down Broadway, the drugstore of New York City, on my way to get a bite to eat. I had not planned nor had any desire to buy a dime bag of coke, but I was easily persuaded to do so. I became paranoid after the first hit. I was so afraid to tell my wife that after almost ten years of abstinence I was back on coke. When I told her, though, she wasn't upset.

We talked about and shared our adulterous encounters with each other, which seemed to break down the barriers between us. I knew deep inside that our behavior would only move me further away from God, but I had gotten to the point where I couldn't stop. I was very angry, bitter, and mean to my wife. I blamed her because she planted the seed by constantly telling me about those parties and all of the fun. In reality it was my fault. I wanted to escape and cocaine, I thought, was my way.

Our marriage was in serious trouble. We drained our joint account and continued to be at each other's throats—so different from the early days when we catered to each other's needs. We used to wear matching outfits as we rode bikes through Central Park. Her brothers thought that I felt I was better than everybody else. But her brothers got to know me, and we respected each other. I wouldn't even dare think of putting my hands on her—though sometimes I really wanted to—because I know her brothers would have killed me. Her brothers were very well known in the hood and maintained a strong reputation.

The madness went on for months though it seemed like years. We now had three children, and the space was very small. I started drinking more to ease the pain, but it didn't help. I truly loved her and didn't want our marriage to fail, but I had school on my plate as well as a stressful job at the market.

Then it happened. I came home from school, and my wife, children, and most of the furniture were gone. I could not believe that she would take the kids and go. I slipped deeper and deeper into depression. I was a broken man but chose not to turn to the God who had brought me out of many dangerous situations.

Weeks before my wife left, someone who was aware that I was a Christian gave me several books. One book in particular was entitled, "If Only He Knew." As I read it, I wept like never before. The book showed me exactly how selfish and cruel I had been to my wife. I know without a doubt that God gave me that book. He wanted me to see myself for what I truly was.

As I read the book, I thought long and hard about the many men who have never realized or was ever shown the error of their ways. They continue to behave in an insane manner because they don't know any better. But it was too late for my marriage, and my wife would not take any responsibility. She blamed everything on me. I knew that as long as she made me totally responsible there was no way that we could make it.

I still was not open to the thought of counseling. I was very lonely in my apartment, in a place of deep despair. I believed that anyone who went to counseling were really crazy. How wrong I was!

One night, my wife's sister knocked on the door. As soon as I opened it, she handed me some papers. Divorce papers. I was blown away, but I signed them only out of fear. I somehow felt that if I didn't sign them that the matter would only get worse. But it got worse anyway because she moved right across the street from me, which was good for the children but very painful for me because I then saw her with other people. One friend of hers wanted to fight me, but I knew that if I hit that girl I probably wouldn't stop. I chose to walk away and drown myself in a bottle of Absolut Vodka, which led me straight to the coke spot. More PMS (pain, misery, and suffering).

I never heard anything further about the divorce, so I decided to find out if it had indeed gone through. In October 1995, I spoke to a lawyer, who found out that I was no longer married.

Although I felt relieved, I will always love and respect her. She has been a tremendous blessing to me.

Let's Do It Again

Before long, I met someone else whom I believed God wanted me to marry. I met Tonia while working on my second master's degree at Mercy College. Prior to meeting her, I had a classmate, Chrissy, who liked me, but I didn't know it. We had several classes together and always sat next to each other. I liked her too but was too afraid to tell her for fear that she would reject me. I told her that I liked Tonia and took her to one of Tonia's classes for her opinion. Big, big mistake! She hardly ever spoke to me again.

I started to talk with Tonia a little more than normal. She too had a good head on her shoulders and also attended church. The only problem was that she was just a church member and not a Christian. I needed someone whom loved God. As I started to get to know her better, we became emotionally and physically intimate, another big mistake. I was still unaware of the bond that sex creates. Tonia had been divorced also, and we shared our marriage stories. I reluctantly told her about my drug problem and was very surprised that she didn't kick me to the curb immediately. She told me that I would soon stop using. I was both surprised and encouraged by her words.

Tonia was well educated and a very studious person. She owned her own condominium, which spoke volumes about her money management skills. I met her in October, and we were engaged four months later. That was too quick, but I was anxious to get away from my ex-wife and the drug scene.

Tonia and I married that June and had the reception in August. Soon several things began to trouble me. One was Tonia

61

didn't like to cook much. She was very much into eating healthy foods and taking care of her body, and I was very ignorant to healthy eating. I had been married to what I would almost call a chef. I ate barbecue chicken, macaroni and cheese, and collard greens with banana pudding for dessert. Rather than learn about and understand Tonia's ways, I became upset.

Tonia was not employed when I met her and that added stress and dissatisfaction for me after we were married. I was used to sharing expenses as opposed to covering expenses.

Tonia's mom, who was an excellent cook, was a very sweet Southern woman who always stayed on Tonia to make sure that I ate. She was always present in our home and had a strong impact on Tonia's actions. I thought that she was too strong and became uncomfortable around her because she dominated my home. My relationship with her became very tense, and we fell out after only a short period of time. I later learned that my own insecurities were to blame. Tonia's mom only wanted the best for us, and I was wrong about her.

I started staying out late and avoiding the sensitive issues. When Tonia and I argued, I left and used. I found every reason to escape and be alone with my medication. I was working with the the Dept. of Education and was able to support my habit. I wanted to be free and not trust anyone with my secret of addiction.

Many people often came to me for comfort and prayer. My pastor didn't understand addiction except for what he had read and studied. It was hard for me to trust him, so I suffered. I moved further and further away from Tonia and from God.

I soon moved out and back to my old apartment. I was very lonely and sad about what appeared to be another failed marriage. At this point in my life, I knew that I had to stop using or die. I reached out for help from my good friend Stan the Man, who was very helpful and supportive. I, however, lost contact with Tonia and our daughter, Nae-Nae.

After a five-year separation, I decided to file for divorce in November. The following February, I met a young, dark chocolate female who was, in my opinion, a dime piece. She worked in the corporate world, was extremely intelligent, and always dressed to the nines. The problem was, she had a sister with the same resume. I didn't know which one to talk, so I chose Claire.

Our first date was a disaster, but I just didn't want to get the message. We dated for three months, and I finally got the courage to tell her that it just wasn't working. She agreed, and we remain good friends to this day. Our relationship was a very good learning experience. She taught me many things that are still helpful for my success.

Not long after we broke up, I went to visit my daughter. I was very sad over the recent breakup and really didn't want a relationship at all. I felt hurt, disappointed, and abandoned. I told Tonia about the relationship. As we talked, I noticed something different about Tonia. To this day I can't say what it was. We talked for about two hours, much longer than I had planned. I had learned to protect myself from other people's energy, but this was good energy. I was very attentive, and for the first time in a long time, Tonia spoke straight from her heart. I left feeling real good.

I needed to talk to somebody with a sound mind, so I called my best friend Artie. During our conversation, I realized that God was changing my heart for Tonia. I knew that if God was doing the work, I could not fight against that which I knew to be of Him.

Artie was very happy and prayerful for me. So was my other friend Mike. I also have a very close spiritual sister in ministry who always prayed that God would restore my marriage. Danita is a true soldier for Jesus and knows the word of prayer. She has counseled many through her own experience and has watched and performed the miraculous.

That August, after being separated for six years, Tonia and I reconciled by the power of God Himself. We are still receiving counseling and now minister to many other married couples. I must say that I've come to love and appreciate her more than ever. Tonia is my wife for life.

God is directing me by the power of the Holy Spirit. I know that God is the ultimate judge of every decision that we make, and He examines our motives. I also realize that I am just His feeble servant and that my knowledge is very limited. I can only make suggestions based on my limited experiences and pray that you will seek divine direction.

Statistics say that half of all marriages fail. Having said that, I strongly suggest that you don't get married until you are totally willing to be committed first to God and then to your mate. The marriage won't last without God's divine presence. Biblically three is indeed the number of completion. Marriage must have three parties in order to survive life's toughest blows and bruises. The Bible states that, "a threefold cord is not easily broken, Ecclesiastes 4:12, KJV God has to tie the knot in every successful marriage.

Don't get married until you have found someone other than your mate to whom you can expose everything, someone who gives you sound guidance based on Scripture. We all need someone to discuss our deepest issues and concerns with. Just make sure the person is professional and godly.

Trusting people is hard, but it's very important to have someone you can be open and honest with. Sometimes people hold everything inside until they finally explode. Remember that whatever is inside of you is bound to come out on you. Better to let it out than have it come out on its own, which can be very dangerous. Please trust me on this one. I know because it happened to me, and I just want to save you and someone else the pain.

Don't get married until you have examined your finances and spending habits. You must communicate with your mate about money, and watch their habits when it comes to giving, spending, and saving. If not discussed and considered early on, it can lead to disaster. One party may want to save while the other is carelessly spending. They say that money is the root of all evil. The truth is, the love of money is the root of all evil, 1 Timothy 6:10, KJV. Consider the many relationships that have failed simply over dollar bills.

Don't get married until you both get tested for any diseases. If you are living a righteous life, this should not be a problem. Yet many Christians fall in the area of sex. In fact, many born-again believers think that it is okay to have sex once in a while.

If your partner is not disease-free, you must decide as to whether or not you can live with that person and their illness. I know many who have partners with illnesses, and they are both very happy. Get tested and make sure that they do too.

Don't get married until you've spent quality time getting to know the person. You are guaranteed to fail if you don't. We live in a very fast-paced society, but you will regret it if you don't go slow. Go slow, and don't have sex. Sex creates a bond that will always damage the relationship.

I strongly suggest you read *The Ten Commandments of Dating,* *by Ben Young and Dr. Samuel Adams.* To me, this book is the bible on sound, strong relationships. I tell all of my students that readers are leaders and leaders are readers. So read.

Don't get married for looks alone. Looks will soon change, sooner than you may think. I once met a very pretty young lady who was gorgeous until she spoke. Then I saw the ugliest monster you could ever imagine. She really was beautiful but spoke like a demon. Again, don't marry because of what a person looks like or has or does.

Don't get married until you have prayed earnestly, seeking the face of God. Then wait for God's answer. He loves you and will lead you if you wait upon Him.

A good friend of mine told me that most people who marry only hear one part of the "for better or worse" line. We always believe that the marriage will only make us better or that together we will enhance each other. That's all good and dandy. I too wish that for every married couple. The reality is that sometimes the opposite happens, sometimes as soon as we say, "I do."

We should be prepared for any situation. We don't want the worst to come, but it can and sometimes does. I know someone who recently got married, and soon after, his wife became ill. He had been saving money, and they both shared the household responsibilities. But before long, every saved dollar was spent just to maintain their basic needs. He had not expected this and was very troubled, to say the least. I had a similar experience while working for the Department of Education. My wife was out of work for several years and all the financial weight was on my shoulders. I handled it about as well as my friend.

Please count all the costs before you say yes. Marriage is one of my greatest life experiences, but because I did not receive the proper guidance and counsel, I paid a tremendous price. Please communicate openly and honestly even when you court and date. I don't suggest that you say too much too soon, but as God leads you to share and listen, do so with an open and discerning spirit.

"Don't Get Married Until You've Tarried"

Don't get married until you've fasted and prayed
Don't get married until before the Lord you've stayed
Don't get married because of looks
Wait 'til you've read all sixty-six books
Don't get married because you feel alone
Spread yourself before God's throne
Then He'll move and you'll get married
But please don't do it until you've tarried.

chapter 7

WHO WILL CARRY THE TORCH?

One thing that I love about the Olympics is the opening ceremony when people from different races and all ages join together to carry the Olympic torch. Every four years, I look forward to watching those long-distance runners—some very well known, others not—pass that brightly lit torch. Each runner depends upon the other to take the torch just a little farther. Imagine what would happen if one runner was not in the right place at the right time!

To me, the torch is symbolic of something special that can be passed down in families from one generation to the next. As I stated in the chapter "Affliction by Addiction," the vicious cycle of addiction is passed down from one generation to the next, but that is not what I'm referring to in this instance. What I am referring to are the many different traits, recipes, and gifts that are passed down from generation to generation.

Who will carry the torch when I've gone to the other side? Will it be Shannel, Kevin, or Naomi? Will it be all three, or none? Will God have to go outside of my lineage for the mantle to continue? This is one of my major concerns with my seed. I love my children. I constantly praise God for the most beautiful children in the world. They have been through so much because of my stubbornness and disobedience. Yet I know that my God strongly desires a Joshua or a Deborah to proclaim His goodness. He has managed, in spite of me, to show my children His awesome greatness. They don't just know *about* God, they *know* Him. They've seen His mighty hand carry me through the worst of life's experiences, whether it was addiction, separation, or divorce, and they saw God keep me in perfect peace. They have also witnessed God's mighty anointing upon me while I'm preaching His Word.

My children have seen me stand silent in the midst of ridicule and persecution from those we all love. They have heard me pray and cry out to God when my own loved ones were cruel and vicious. God has granted me the ability to raise not one but three precious gifts that He has placed under my care. I must be accountable for them. We've had some real good, funny, nurturing days, but we have also had days that I am ashamed of. Through each experience, the Lord has been a present help. This is the legacy I leave for future family members to remember and consider.

The Bible gives us many examples of the importance of torch carriers. The chosen people of God were often told to remind their descendants of God's miraculous works. He did not want them to forget how He brought them through, He and He alone.

God always raised up a torch carrier. One of my favorites was Joshua, who closely followed Moses and submitted to his leadership. I honestly believe that Joshua had no idea what God had in store for him. He just stayed faithful and walked in submission to God. When Moses died, Joshua was immediately called to take on the leadership role. The torch was passed to him, and he was in the right position to receive it.

I thank God for Joshua's example of true humility, which took him to his position of leadership. Joshua saw God's hand at work in Moses and trusted the same awesome God to see him through. As a result, he was given the highest calling in life: to lead God's chosen people into the Promised Land. He carried the torch and held it high. Joshua was followed closely by Caleb, and the torch continued to pass.

God has called me into ministry, and I often wonder which one of my children will carry the torch.

My first born, Shannel Michelle, knows God and is clear that God has a tremendous call on her life. She has, I believe, suffered the most through all of the difficulties, which can work in her favor but could also be a hindrance. She can allow God to use every negative experience for His glory, for He does that well. Or she can allow those negative experiences to hinder her anointing and sabotage God's strong hand of victory and deliverance. I know that she will trust God. The Devil says otherwise, but he is a liar. Shannel will carry the torch, so I continue to pray and praise God for that which I may never see. I believe that by faith Shannel is a mighty warrior who will touch the lives of many.

Kevin Terence, Jr., or as he is called, has experienced many hardships as a child. He too encountered the pain of two parents separating at a young age. He has witnessed the blows and bondage that the Devil uses to kill entire families. Yet he also survived. Kevin is truly a soldier. God has handpicked him to encourage me in my darkest hours of despair, shame, and guilt. He was only eleven years old when I heard some of the most encouraging words that a child could ever say. He said, "Dad, I love you, and I'm with you no matter what." He called me a winner at the worst time of my life. How could he know? I cried uncontrollably then, and I get goose bumps now just recalling that day. Only God could have given him those divine words, and Kevin had the choice to obey in sharing them or not. Thank God that he made the right choice. I needed those words bad and only God knew how bad. Kevin showed me his ability to obey God even at a young age. All of my neighbors commend me on these two beautiful, respectful, and well-mannered children. To God be the glory.

Kevin like Shannel is very, very intelligent. He has been academically inclined since his early years and is also very humorous—maybe too humorous. His humor works in his favor but can easily cause him or others much pain. Unfortunately, he got it from me.

Kevin's God-given abilities afford him the opportunity to be mightily used for God's glory. He really broke my heart when he fathered a child at the age of twenty with a schoolmate. I often ask myself how many times have I broken his and Shannel's heart by not being present when they needed me most? I have forgiven him as almighty God continues to forgive me. I love all of my children just as God shows me daily His grace and mercy.

My third child's name alone speaks of God's awesome joy and continuous presence: Naomi Kayla Shekinah Deborah Hodge. Nae Nae, as I call her, is just something special. She was born during my greatest hours of adversity. Drugs, depression, work demands, and a rushed-into marriage resulted from Nae Nae's unplanned birth.

Although I was present at each child's birth, Naomi's was the scariest, as she was a C-section. Tonia needed me, but I thought that drugs were more important (the power of addiction). Thank God for freedom from active addiction. From day one, Nae Nae stole my heart. She came out looking just like Ma and Shannel. What a combination! I was sprung. We nicknamed her Honey Bunny. Shannel and Kevin were Scooter and Skeeter, or Scoot-Skeet.

Nae Nae was breast fed and nurtured early with gospel and classical music even as a newborn. She is brilliant. I recall her singing "Seasons" at age two. Tonia was very wise and caring with Nae Nae even when she was in the womb, and we prayed for her as I rubbed Tonia's stomach. I really knew that it had a lot to do with God's presence and hand on her little life. She is kind, humble, and beautiful. She has Shannel's beautiful looks and Mom's kind heart.

I said that I have three children, but there are two more children whom I dare not exclude: Starlene and Lawrenson Isaiah. Although these two are not my biological children, they are still mine, as God has entrusted me with their nurturing and upbringing and are precious gifts to me. They love the Lord and also know of His mighty love and power. They have also been scarred by father-absence and the many other struggles and pains of single parenting. Both mothers did really well, in spite of life's circumstances, and the results still remain to this day. Starlene and Lawrenson are doing well and know the richness of almighty God's grace and peace. They are studious, make sound decisions, and have the potential to be greatly used for the glory of God and the souls of men.

So who will carry the torch? Who will dare to trust God with his or her whole life? Who will love and reverence God's holy Word enough to say, "Here I am, send me"? Who is willing to learn the cost of unselfish prayer and to pay such a high price for the millions who are in need?

My prayer is that I have given my children in some portion a measure of God's hope that they will also carry the heavy, humbling torch of the awesome almighty God.

chapter 8
THE GODSENDS

Throughout the many difficult times in my life, God always sent someone to help me. Even my wife has acknowledged how God has used many people to help me in some capacity. I call these people "The Godsends," as they definitely didn't come from the Devil. God touched their hearts to help and guide me at crucial points in my life. I would not classify The Godsends as friends, as they have come and gone; they were only there for a season.

I was about ten years old when I asked one of the after-school counselors, Dexter, for a quarter, and he gave me eighteen cents. Since that worked, I asked him again. He told me that I could wash his mother's car for spare change. This went on for years. Dexter had no ill motives and never tried anything funny. My friends and I would wash that car for five dollars at a time when money was real hard to come by. He was truly a godsend. I don't know whatever happened to Dexter, but I will always remember him. At that point in my life, I could have started stealing and robbing, but he was there. I had a car-washing job that helped me through the rough times.

Another godsend was my fifth grade teacher. She always went the extra mile to make sure that all of her students learned what she taught. I remember that class so well because I was in the fifth grade and still didn't know my multiplication tables. My teacher encouraged another student to work with me for three weeks.

At the end of the three-week period, my classmate and I stood in front of the classroom as our fellow classmates asked us multiplication questions from the table from one through twelve. We answered every question correctly. At the end of the quiz, our teacher gave us five dollars to split, and we bought a hero sandwich. That was the best hero I have ever tasted.

My teacher also took the class on many trips that she paid for out of her own pocket. She suggested that we visit the planetarium on weekends. At the end of the year, she gave each student the exact carfare to and from the museum based on our free ticket stubs, as nobody paid for the subway at that time.

Fast Eddie was a real godsend. When I got kicked out of high school, he helped me secure my first full-time job as a messenger that paid two dollars and fifty cents an hour. That was like a million dollars to a young black dropout with very little skills. Fast Eddie taught me how to do many other things on that job, so I got several raises. He was in my life for only a short period, but he had a strong impact. He was a very humorous fellow and saw the good in all things. He made me laugh and really showed me a side of life that I will always appreciate.

Another guy who was instrumental during my teenage years was Token-Face Harold. Around that time, tokens had a Y-shape in the center, and Harold had a Y-shape just beneath his lips. Hence his name.

I remember walking into the supermarket one Saturday and Harold watching me as I picked out my favorite apple pie, called Tasty Pie, which cost twenty-five cents. Harold asked me if I wanted to work. Before he finished his sentence, I was answering yes. My job was to pick the items and then deliver them to the customer's address. I worked for tips. There was no commission except for a Tasty Pie every once in a while. Harold saw something in me that I didn't see in myself. He trusted me and gave me a responsible task.

I had to collect the money on arrival and bring every dime back to the store. Although I made fun of Harold, I was very grateful. That job led me to my next job, which was selling newspapers every Sunday. I truly believe that if you open yourself up, God will use other people in your time of greatest need. If He did it for me, I know that He can and will do it for you.

Sarah Moore was another person who left an impression on my life that will last for all eternity. Our meeting was truly divine. I had just given my heart to the Lord when my good friend and neighbor had gotten shot. He didn't die but was in very bad shape. His room was next door to my kitchenette. We shared food but really had little or none left. I was only making one hundred dollars a week, and my rent was sixty-five dollars.

I told Sister Moore about the incident. Several days after my friend's release from the hospital, she took us shopping and bought us two hundred dollars worth of groceries. She also paid my friend's rent for several months.

There was something about that lady that I'll never forget. I didn't know what that something was, but I wanted it. She was the boldest lady I had ever met. She really loved God and was a trooper, a warrior, and a true lover of the souls of humankind. There was nothing that she would not do, no place she would not go, and no money she would not spend to help anyone experience God's love for them. Sister Moore was ridiculed and often verbally abused, but she refused to be deterred from her mission. Her middle name was Going, and boy, did she love to go. She held dearly to the cross and lived on the battlefield.

Sarah was my greatest spiritual mentor as well as my favorite spiritual mom. She gave me more than any Bible school or study, as she poured herself into me. Her home-going service was my first happy/sad funeral. I was sad to lose her but overjoyed because I knew on the inside that she had made it into heaven. Sarah Moore was directly sent by God Almighty for my enhancement.

I spoke earlier about my pastor, Dr. John L. Scott, but must say more. When it comes to individuals who have touched and blessed my life, Dr. Scott stands very high on the mountain of many. He would probably not approve of my placing him only a few levels below Christ. He has been and still is a tremendous asset to my life and any success that I have achieved. He always saw the best in me even when I was blinded by the many distractions of life. From day one, he was there.

I remember the day that I had received a nice amount of money from the IRS. I gave the church a decent offering and told Dr. Scott that I would see him in a couple of weeks. I was going to hang out awhile. As soon as I came back to the church, he called all of the church mothers, and in the middle of the service, he called me to the altar, and they all laid hands on me. I was so angry yet grateful at the same time. I was embarrassed then, but his method sure worked.

Dr. Scott always encouraged my heart. In my deepest, darkest moments, he was always there with a word of hope. I've watched that man go out of his way and dig in his pocket to assist many. He was there for me when my own dad was absent. He too is a trooper and is very big on education. He's the type of pastor who does not look for accolades or recognition. He has a true heart.

Dr. Scott is a giver and has given himself to many people. When my mother was sick and we started to plan the funeral, Dr. Scott stopped us and gave us hope beyond sight. My mother got better and went on to graduate from college. Dr. Scott even witnessed in an airplane at forty thousand feet to a man who was facing life in prison. Dr. Scott encouraged him and interceded on his behalf. The man gave his heart to Christ in midair and later received another chance at life. He was free! What a godsend!

Troy (Big Nick) Smith is also a godsend. Troy and I grew up together. I was a little older and never considered how that young man would touch and encourage my heart. In our adulthood, we reconnected and worked together for several years. We always go in and out of touch, but he is my friend forever.

I had just experienced the most embarrassing, shameful, and humiliating moments of my life. When I finally got released from that jail cell, I was suicidal. I began to check my voicemails, although I really didn't want to. I listened to nine messages that only tripled the pain I was already feeling. And then it happened. The last message was from Troy. His words went straight to the depths of my oh-so-dark and heavy heart. "I can't wait to see and hear the testimony that God is going to give you through this one." Those words didn't just touch my heart, they saved my life. Troy was indeed a godsend.

Bonnie Blue was also a godsend. She was my supervisor on a job. Bonnie didn't just hire me, she took me under her wing and taught me so much. She suggested that I return to school so that she might promote me to a much-esteemed position. I didn't think that I was doing that well on the job, but Bonnie saw something in me. That lady treated me like royalty, which made the other workers were envious. Although I didn't realize my full potential, she surely inspired me.

John G is another godsend who was used in a grand way to inspire me. I was an active runner for years, but I slipped into a depression and began to eat anything and everything. I gained weight and completely lost the desire to run. I saw John one day as he was returning from a race that I had run the previous year. We started to discuss running, and I told him that I had run three New York City Marathons. John told me that I should start running again. I brushed him off, but he was persistent. He registered me for a five-mile race and paid for it. That was the turning point for me. The next year, I ran over ten races and qualified for the NYC Marathon and the NYC Half-Marathon. John and I remain good friends and continue to train together. He has also introduced me to many others who share our passion for running and healthy living. What a person!

There have been many other godsends who have contributed to my life who are not named here. But you know who you are. You are the Mother Blands and the Christopher Michaels who have helped in ways you may never know. You are the sisters, brothers, and colleagues in Christ who deposited so much of yourselves into my life so that I might have a positive impact on the world. Even if for only a moment, you were right there. You are a godsend.

chapter 9

I BELIEVE IN YOU

One of the most profound statements a dear friend made to me years ago still resounds loud in my heart, "Kevin, I believe in you." It was the turning point for me at a time of deep despair. What her words said to me was, "Although you might not see it now, feel it now, or even want it, I believe *for* you." My friend was not bound by "it's all about me." She was able to sense my need and ministered to it.

There are times in life when our vision is so unclear that we need others to see for us. Thank God for those who became my eyes when the circumstances of life blinded me. I believe that anyone can obtain success with the help of another's confidence in them. My friend's words came just before my life-changing experience by the hand of the almighty God, which at that time was through song. God used worldly songs to draw me to Himself. He sang words like, all this love is waiting for you.

It was not my friend who spoke nor the songs. It was God the Redeemer. He spoke to me, saying, "Kevin, I Am Who I Am believes in you. Don't focus on the past or the pain. Don't hold onto bitterness and stay at the pity party. I know you and, most of all, I love you. Kevin, I see in you that which you cannot see. I see you as a servant, a leader. I see you not only as a servant and a leader, but most important, I see you as My son. You are Mine if you want Me. All of My riches are yours, no matter what you've been through, no matter how deep the scars may be, I am your healer."

God then sent people, signs, and songs. Imagine that the Creator of this universe would be so concerned with me! I had become mean, angry, and very rebellious, but He still believed in me. He saw me working with seniors. He saw me teaching children and adults out of pure love—His love. God saw me counseling drug addicts even when I was on drugs. When I was at the worst point in my life, He saw me as I am today. He saw me as a writer with a strong desire to encourage as many people as He will allow.

God saw my heart transformed by the power of the Holy Spirit. He believed in me so much that He changed me and He saved me from destitution, destruction, and death.

In November 2001, I went to a marathon. Not just any marathon—the New York City Marathon, one of the greatest events in the city. The marathon attracts some thirty-five thousand runners and a million spectators. I had just started running again and told my friend that I wanted to run the marathon.

We were in Harlem somewhere around mile twenty-three. My friend suggested that I join the race, so I did. As soon as I started to run, I met a guy named Pete from Brazil. I will never forget Pete or what he said to me, "Thanks for joining the race, Kevin. Now you can help me finish the race." I thought that he needed my help, so I said, "Sure, Pete. No problem."

Pete and I ran through Harlem, but by the time we got to 59th Street, I was done. I had on too many clothes and was exhausted. I told Pete to go on ahead. He said, "Kevin, I'm not leaving you."

He locked his arm into mine, and together we completed the race. Pete believed in me enough to help me all the way to the end.

I was so overjoyed that I cried and told Pete that I would never forget him. He in turn kept thanking *me*. The following year, I ran fifteen races and qualified for the NYC Marathon. I have since run three marathons and over ten halves only because somebody believed in me.

The Bible states in Hebrews 11 that faith is the substance of things hoped for and the evidence of things not seen. Faith is the stuff, matter, and material that has brought me thus far, but it wasn't always my faith. Many times, it was someone else's; some other person who was able to see what I could not. My faith came from God and only increased as I trusted Him and stood on His holy Word. Each answered prayer encouraged me to believe in Him for more.

A good friend once told me that if God brings you to something, He will certainly bring you through it. I try to remember those words in time of adversity. Each trying circumstance and situation has taught me to believe in Him to lead, guide, and see me through.

I stated in the last chapter that at one point in my life I was suicidal. The only thing that kept me alive was God speaking to me through a message from my friend Troy on voicemail. He knew exactly where I was and the pain I was in. No one else stood with me that night, for whatever reasons. But God was, and He carried me through the night safely. He even allowed me to get much-needed rest. Then He woke me up in the morning and continued carrying me for months. He used three people to encourage my soul. Three people who believed in me at a rough time in my life.

This book is really not about me. Although you've read a number of chapters about my life from the harsh beginning until now, this book is not for my purposes or glorification. I wrote this book because I believe in *you*! I believe that you are worth every minute, hour, day, week, and month that was put into writing. This book was penned with you at heart.

The sole purpose for my writing this book is so that you can know that, wherever you are in life, this former drug user, dealer, alcoholic, and now college graduate believes in you. I do believe that no matter what arrows, darts, or daggers have been hurled at you, you are able to rise up and be exactly the person God sees in you. I believe that the same merciful, compassionate, and considerate Savior is ready to meet you right at the point of your need. If you can't believe it, I believe for you. As a matter of fact, you can forget that believe in you. But please don't forget that God believes in you. He knows where you are and exactly what you've been through. He loves you more than you could ever imagine. The power of God will turn your darkest night into bright sunshine. His ability is infinite and his Word is sure. He has promised that if you just trust Him, He will see you through.

"I Believe In You"

I believe in you though you may not
God is looking inside and he sees a lot
A lot of potential and things you possess
He has always promised to bring you the best
In spite of your tests and all you've been through
God has the power to make you anew
He loves you so much and His Word is true
I believe in you

Don't Go Too Far

Please don't go too far, stay away too long, or come back too late to experience His amazing grace. Even after I received His goodness, I managed to walk away from Him. He promoted me in many positions. I had a career that someone with my background could only dream about. And God had elevated me to a place spiritually that I never considered. Yet for a season, I turned my back for another taste of worldly pleasure. But in His great grace and mercy, God brought me back to Himself. The price for my straying was a very high one, and today I am still paying it.

Don't stay where you are if it is not of Him. You don't have to. If you can't get out, it's okay because He will bring you out and into Himself. Please don't let it be too late. There is a point of no return. It has happened to many and still does today. Just draw near to Him, and He will draw near to you. Ask God to help you believe for that which you do not and cannot see. One of the most profound prayers in the Bible is, "Lord, I do believe, help thou my unbelief."

God has been waiting for you to trust Him for a long time. The worst thing that you can do is rob yourself of that which God has for you, and this is worse than being robbed by someone else. Sure there's a devil, and his main objective is to kill, steal, and destroy you, but God is greater. His promises are true. You can bank on them.

I am in your corner, rooting just for you. I encourage you because I remember my story everyday. I can't forget you, and I refuse to allow you to stay where you are. I believe in you.

"First You Must Trust"

First you must trust, and then you will see
He will do good for you like He's done unto me.
Please don't forget to remember and always recall
The power of God and His love for us all.
From the Lord I have learned to always be nice
And when I see trouble be good and think twice
Joy, wisdom, knowledge, and college are all meant for us
But first you must trust.

chapter 10
FROM DOPE TO HOPE

I've always enjoyed the privilege of traveling from one place to another. There are so many ways to travel now that makes it more exciting. I recently took a trip overseas. Many people frowned at the fact that the trip was such a great distance. I knew that I would spend a great deal of time traveling, but it didn't bother me. I was too thrilled with the purpose of the trip to engage myself in negative energy.

I always love the feeling of achievement when I finish a race. Between point A and point B are many struggles and obstacles. I've seen others who just could not complete the race for various reasons. They started well and planned to get to the other side but didn't make it. They stopped or were forced to stop somewhere between the two points, the start and the finish.

I started at dope and am now at hope. I started out with two parents, whom I truly love, who at young ages were afflicted and addicted to dope. I don't blame them for their plight in this thing called life. I did before because of my ignorance and limited knowledge. And I blamed many others as well. I was angry at God, whom at that time I didn't know, and I blamed the whole world. I was deep inside the belly of dope and allowed it to reside deep inside of me. What a nasty, filthy place, but that is where I made my home. The rent was free, but the utility bill almost killed me. For many years, I was stuck on stupid.

Then one day someone told me that I didn't have to stay there any longer. But I still needed to get to the start line. The good thing is that now I was in motion. I crawled, walked, and then started running out. As I began to move forward, I knew that I needed to pace myself. I needed a coach because I was moving from the familiar to the unknown. I needed someone who knew the route and all the rest stops. I was wounded and scarred very deeply, so I also needed a physician.

Because my parents were still bound, they could not speak up for me, so I needed an advocate. The minute that I started to move, I heard voices accusing me of the many wrongs that I committed, so I needed a lawyer also. Would you believe that I was told that I could find an all-inclusive person, Jesus? I was assured that everything I needed was in Him. So I decided to give Him a chance to prove Himself to me. He did and is still doing exactly that.

Prior to receiving Christ Jesus as my Savior, I listened to Jehovah Witnesses, Muslims, and my best friend, who was a Five Percenter. I listened to them all, but not one of those religions emphasized love. And love was what I needed, and I needed it real bad. I heard things like "Don't eat pork," "the white man is the devil," and I was even told that I was God. The love that I've experienced is almost incomprehensible. It is very hard to explain but so easy to receive if desired.

I was instantly transformed from dope to hope. Although I didn't instantly stop smoking cigarettes, I did stop drinking and smoking pot. There was something new about me, and others took notice. I was hope come true, or hope actualized. I was in a new place, full of joy and peace. This hope has taken me to dangerous street corners, shelters, and prisons with words of life. This hope that I've experienced is light in the darkest tunnel. It is a refuge in the time of storm. Just imagine living a seemingly defeated life for twenty-one years and suddenly your change comes. The breaker comes and all walls start tumbling down. You move from point A suddenly, rapidly, and before you can even blink, you're at point B.

Most of this book shares my story of pain, misery, and suffering, but I must say it was worth every disappointment and every tear. I still have a lot of regret for past behavior and for those who were affected by it. Some still hold onto my past behavior and refuse to forgive me even though I have offered my apologies for many years. But I understand and am okay because I'm in hope now. I am enjoying the journey. I've been brought out of darkness and into the marvelous light. Each day is a new reward. Today in hope, I have gratitude and a better attitude. I've been freed from those heavy chains of darkness and bondage.

I recall talking to a friend who attended my graduation from college with my second master's degree. He told me that he was happy for me but didn't think that it could happen to him. I told him as I tell you and anyone else who wants to achieve success, if God did it for a dope addict like me, He can do it for anyone in the world. Anyone who desires change can have change. They told me to change or I would be begging for change. I couldn't change, but I found the Changer, and His name is Jesus. He can change any situation. God loves you and has a marvelous plan for you. It's free, and yet it costs. You can't buy it; you just simply open your heart to receive God. He does not force His way in, as He is indeed a gentle but firm Savior.

My hope is not just for money, property, or prestige. My hope is for the glory of God and the souls of men, which is already the finished work of Christ. My hope is based solely and wholly on God's immutable Word. I look forward to life after this one.

I know a young lady who met a nice young man. He was so attracted to her that he asked what he could do for her. She told him that she wanted to live forever. He walked away very sad and disappointed because he could not fulfill her request. But I know someone who can grant that request. You can live forever with God. Today, I have received a living hope and a sure salvation, and so can you. God can carry anyone who desires to go from dope to hope.

"From Dope to Hope"

From dope to hope He brought me from
It's by His love and grace that to this place I've come
So while I'm here I must reflect and give him all the glory
For allowing me to honestly share with you my story
I'm grateful now though things may come,
I've found a way to cope
It's through His peace that will never cease
I've come from dope to hope.

How I got from dope to hope all lies in the power of God's greatest gift of salvation. If you don't know anything about salvation, let me give you some divine wisdom.

What I Believe about Salvation

Taken from Reverend Hodge's
Credo Statement for Ordination
December 2001

When I first came to church, I often heard people say that I needed to be saved. I knew for a fact that my life was out of control. I knew that I was sad and miserable but I did not have any notion of what it meant to be saved.

I started attending church on a regular basis. I even sang in the choir, but I still did not know what it meant to be saved. I gave my heart to the Lord and accepted Jesus Christ as my personal Lord and Savior, but I still did not have any idea what being saved truly meant. I was able to quote John 3:16, but I still did not have an understanding of God's wonderful plan of salvation. I just didn't comprehend God's ways.

Because of man's rebelliousness and disobedience, he became separated from the presence of God and lost. God sought a way to reestablish a close relationship with man—this is called God's wonderful plan of salvation. Salvation is freedom from the power and penalty of sin. Salvation can only come through one accepting the finished and completed work of Jesus Christ, the Son of the living God.

According to the New American Heritage Dictionary, the word *salvation* means to be delivered from some sort of difficulty. The Holy Bible teaches us in Romans 3:23, "That all have sinned and come short of the glory of God." This means that no one is able to measure up to God's standards of living a holy and sanctified life. Salvation is exactly what Christ had in mind when He left the presence of the most Holy God and stripped Himself of all heavenly glory and took on the form of a servant

(Philippians 2:9–12). Jesus Christ, is, was, and forever will be the way to complete fellowship with God.

Salvation is God extending his undeserving love to anyone and everyone who will receive it. Salvation is the pure demonstration of God's amazing grace. It is God giving and granting us that which we by no means deserve. Salvation comes directly from God's heart of love and mercy and cannot be earned. It is not something that one can work for, buy, or gain. Salvation means to be saved from the power, or domination, of sin.

The Holy Bible states that because of one man's disobedience, all others became sinners (Romans 5:17). Adam, who was the first man that God created, chose to deliberately go against God's truth. Although we are aware that Eve was tempted first, we also know that Adam had knowledge of God's divine will. God told Adam that he could eat from any tree except the Tree of Knowledge of Good and Evil. Adam was the one that caused all to be separated from God, but God had a plan. He planned to bring man back to right relationship and fellowship with Himself. This was the beginning of God's awesome plan of salvation.

Salvation began in the garden of Eden when God searched for Adam. Adam was afraid and hid because he realized that he was naked. He realized that he had been disobedient to God's perfect will. God had plans to only bless, strengthen, and enhance man's life, but when Adam went in the opposite direction of God's will, he became lost, lonely, and miserable. God, who is the source of peace, power, and love, decided to bring man back unto Himself. This began God's wondrous plan of salvation.

But God needed someone who was pure and sinless. He needed someone who had no sin, but we all have sinned. Thank God for the Son of God, Jesus Christ our Lord. He said that He would go and redeem humanity, that He would pay the high price for our sin. The Holy Bible states in Romans 6:23, "The penalty for sin is death." This means that all humanity will have to die because all of us are guilty of sin. Everyone deserves to die because everyone was born in sin (Psalm 51:5). But Jesus came to Earth and subjected Himself to the pain and penalty. He suffered for all of us. "The just for the unjust, the good for the bad." He made a way when there seemed to be no way. Jesus promises not just life here but he also offers eternal life with Him.

The gospel of John explains it all, for it tells the story in such a way that even a young child can comprehend the message of God's awesome love with the help of the Holy Spirit. John 3:16 is as clear when it says, "For God so loved the world that He gave His only begotten Son, that whosoever believeth in Him should not perish but have everlasting life." Salvation is having a relationship with Jesus Christ. Salvation is having a new life in Christ. It is not religion but a lifestyle. It is abundant life. Salvation is the privilege of knowing God and walking in His ways.

In conclusion, there was a very famous singer who shared these words: "If salvation was something that money could buy, the rich would live and the poor would die." Thank God that salvation is His demonstration of true love in action. Salvation is liberation; it is coming out of darkness into God's marvelous love and light. It is trusting in the light of the world, Jesus Christ.